I HAVE BETTER PLANS FOR YOU

"LIFE IS FULL OF OPPORTUNITIES
TO LEARN, GROW & HEAL"

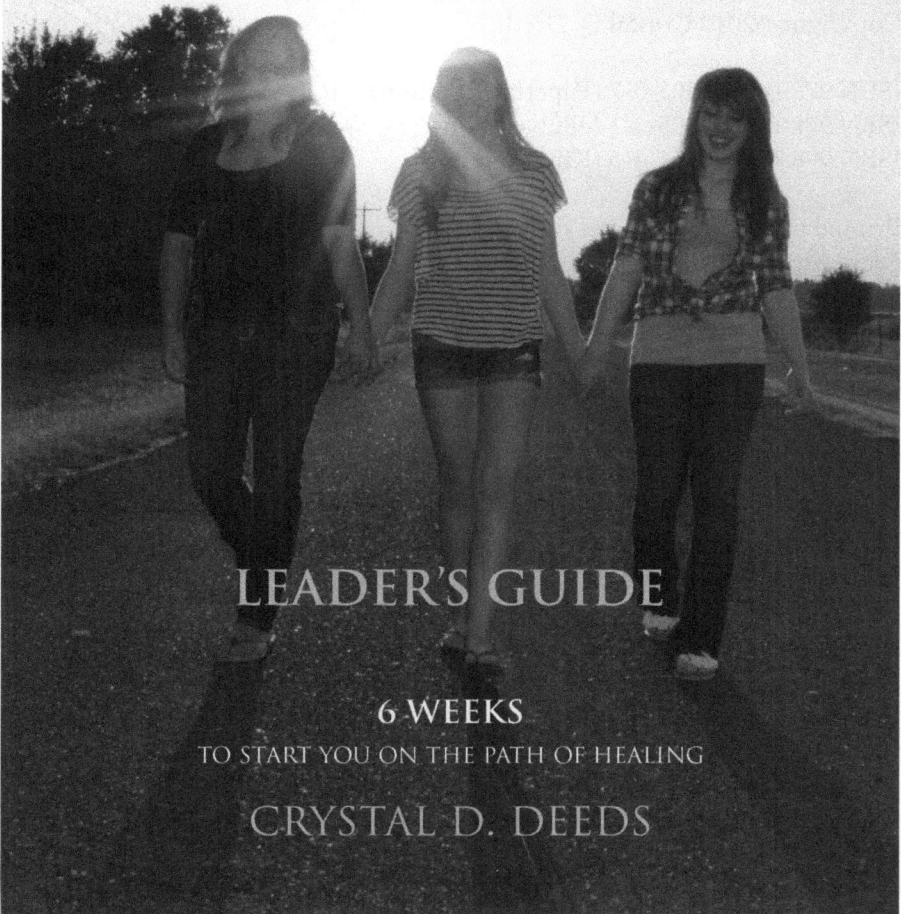

LEADER'S GUIDE

6 WEEKS
TO START YOU ON THE PATH OF HEALING

CRYSTAL D. DEEDS

I Have Better Plans for You
LEADER'S GUIDE
Copyright ©2013 Crystal D. Deeds

ISBN 978-0-9859505-0-7 (Paperback edition)
ISBN 978-0-9859505-2-1 (ePub edition)
ISBN 978-0-9859505-4-5 (Kindle edition)

Printed in the United States of America
Set in Minion Pro

Published in association with H.O.P.E. Ministries
Requests for information should be communicated through
www.betterplansfor.me or
ihavebetterplansforyou@gmail.com

Cover design by Love Lion Studio and Aubrey Harper
www.lovelionstudio.com

Testimonials

"For I know the plans I have for you," declares the LORD, "plans to prosper you and not to harm you, plans to give you hope and a future." Jeremiah 29:11

God does have better plans for you! His plans include a hope and a future. He would never bring you harm; nor will He allow those who have to go unpunished. God loves you and like any loving father, He does not want you to live with the pain and resentment that often comes in life.

I have known Crystal Deeds for years as her pastor and friend. I can say that she has successfully journeyed through some dark valleys and is willing to walk alongside you in these pages. This is not a book to flip through and sit on the shelf. This is a tool. A guide. A manual for future reference. As one of the sections are titled, healing is a lifelong process.

"I Have Better Plans for You" is an excellent foundation to help you on your way to living a life free from the paralyzing pain from your past. My prayer is that through the wisdom and experience Crystal shares, you too will find healing, hope and God's plans for your future.

Keith Boyer, Former Lead Pastor
Crossroads Community Church
Commerce City, Colorado

"I have been in the ministry over 28 years, visited more than 26 countries, and lived in 4. Over the years my family has seen and experienced enough to know this is a broken world full of broken lives. Crystal has experienced both hurt and healing and been a source of healing to many. I have heard it said a message from the head will reach the head, and a message from the heart will reach the heart, but a message from a life will reach a life. In this book Crystal shares life changing principles from her own life. Anyone would find this book practical, insightful, and helpful; but if you have been deeply hurt or broken or know someone who has, this book can lay a course for healing and wholeness. I personally know Crystal's story and can say she has been through the fire and doesn't even smell like smoke. Let her life story change yours or someone you love who is hurting. I KNOW that the principles and the life shared in this book can bring healing. My prayer is that you will experience it and pass it on. Is. 61:1-4"

Jon Eastlick, Outreach Pastor
Crossroads Community Church
Freeport, Illinois

"I am glad that I had the opportunity to go through the small group study using this book. It took me to deeper parts in my life, some things that I had buried inside for years and it brought them to the surface and also brought so much healing to my life. The questions and discussions make you think, confess, and share your thoughts. I grew so much from this experience by talking and bringing out the things that needed to come out. I received a new outlook on life, more confidence in myself, and newfound encouragement. I discovered I don't have to let the past experiences of my life keep me from being the person God wants me to be. Sometimes we tend to hold on to the hurtful things in our past and we don't let it go. We also let the enemy lie to us and say that we can never be a good person or that the past has tainted us so we can't live a productive life. The study helped me to realize I had been listening to the enemy's lies and allowing him to steal my joy, so I had to work to change that and start being more aware of when he puts those lies in my head and resist them. This book, with the help of Crystal and God, helped me to let go of the past and, in doing so, I found healing, restoration, and I now know that my life has value and purpose." Teresa (small group participant)

Dedication

This book is dedicated to my mother, Carol.

Introduction

Please allow me the opportunity to tell you a little about myself, my family and this book.

Having been born into a dysfunctional environment, I had very little exposure to church. However, at the age of 4, during an Easter service at my Grandmother's church, I accepted Christ. I remember making the decision based on the promise of receiving a little cloth bible that I could pin to my dress. What a motivation!

Regardless of such a simple, childish motivation, I truly believe that Jesus entered my life at that moment and I can see how He has placed many circumstances and people in my life to draw me closer to Him, this is something I am extremely grateful for.

Foreground: The author, on the day she accepted the Lord. Notice the bible pinned to her dress.
Background: The authors sister, Dee.

I fully accepted and committed my life to Christ at the age of 17. At that pivotal moment, my life began to change drastically.

I married my High School sweetheart at the age of 19, and we have now been married 25 years. He is a wonderful, God fearing man and an amazing, loving Father to our two children. Being married so young has definitely had its challenges, but the two of us have grown together in our relationship with the Lord and that has been the foundation that we have built our family on.

As I mentioned, we have two children, a 23 year old son who is a musician and graphic designer, and a daughter who is 16 and currently in high school. Both of our children, I am pleased to say, have a strong love for the Lord. I am truly blessed and thankful for the support my husband and children have been to me while writing this book.

The process of writing this book began almost 20 years ago when it was impressed upon me to write a book about my life. I tried many times over those years to complete the task to no avail. In fact, each and every time that I would try I inevitably ended up trashing the whole thing; I guess the timing just wasn't right. Then, after several failed attempts, I finally began to write the book you now hold in your hands.

I suppose that writing was easier this time around because I had finally learned the lessons that God wanted me to learn and, most importantly I believe, had seen the process of healing take place in my own life and so I could now share this information with others as well. In other words, I actually had something to say. So, instead of simply being a book about my life, it also became a book about my healing and the steps I had to take to get there.

The healing I experienced in my life was just between the two of us, God and I. with Him guiding me through it step by step. It was tedious and slow, but I truly believe if the process had gone too quickly, I wouldn't have learned as much from it.

The steps I learned through the healing process became something I naturally shared with other hurting individuals, especially in my church youth group. As a youth leader, I was able to use what I had learned to help girls struggling to cope with their own pain and suffering. Helping people find healing became my passion.

The writing of this book has puzzled, challenged, and at the same time forced me to truly see the complexities of the healing process. I am not a Professional Counselor, nor do I hold any degrees or have any extensive training. What I do have, however, is life experience, a personal relationship with my Heavenly Father, a saving relationship with His Son, and the work of the

Holy Spirit in my life, along with several years of experience working with teens in Youth Ministry.

During my years in Youth Ministry I found one thing to be very certain, all pain is pain no matter "to what degree" or how "extreme" it is. No matter the cause, we can never understand the depth of another person's pain because it is only known to God and the individual. We can do our best to sympathize and show compassion to the one who is hurting, but we will not be able to truly comprehend what they are feeling. Each person has a different story to tell and showing compassion and love to them is the best way to help facilitate healing in their life, no matter what they need healing from.

Personally, I am amazed at the complexity of the problems that affect our youth today. In my own small group of girls there were so many different hurts and struggles that at times I wept for the unregenerate world. Just to give an example of the extremes, some of the girls I have worked with have experienced feelings of abandonment due to divorce or lack of parental involvement. Others have suffered sexual and physical abuse most of their lives only to move on to experience the pain of sexual promiscuity, and self-mutilation by various means, as they began trying to find their true identity and worth. No matter what the problem is, one thing is painfully evident; they are all feeling the effects of sin in this world.

As you read this book I will share bits and pieces of my personal testimony and others in order to demonstrate how God facilitated healing in my life and the students that I have worked with. This is by no means "The" manual for healing. I can only pray that it will somehow help to give hope and direction for those who are hurting. I realize that everyone's path to healing is going to vary from mine but I truly believe that the steps are the same no matter how they may look for the individual. Complete Physical, Emotional, and Spiritual healing is a process that will come in layers, steps, and times of rest and release. No matter what you are struggling with, whether it be rejection, hopelessness, abuse, addictions, and beyond, the steps in this book will begin to guide you through the healing process and equip you for a life of freedom.

May God bless you as you work through this book, and may your life experience the freedom that comes from complete healing. Ultimately, I pray that you find hope in the knowledge that God has better plans for you.

Table of Contents

How to Use This Book

Healing is a choice; you will get out of this study exactly what you put in to it. As you let yourself connect to the stories of hurts, habits, and hang-ups, search deep within yourself to find areas in your life that you need to heal.

You may have never been sexually abused, but have you ever had something happen that shook the very foundation of trust and security within your world? You may have never considered suicide, but have you ever felt unwanted, unloved, or abandoned? Have you ever been overwhelmed with hopelessness? As you read through the book and do the study questions try to relate to the foundational messages within the stories so that you can get as much out of them as possible and find the healing you've been looking for.

Each chapter within the book is broken up into smaller "titled" sections, and includes an untitled Intro section at the beginning of each chapter. Chapters are intended to be completed in one week if used independently but may take longer in a small group setting. Each chapter is labeled by week and each section within the chapter is labeled by the day. Be sure to follow the daily reading assignments. In other words, try not to do a marathon reading session in order to read through the entire week in one day. Instead set aside time each day to read the daily section and then throughout the day try to process what you've read so that you can get more out of it.

For your convenience, you will also find a "To Do" list at the beginning of each chapter which includes a check off list for the daily reading, study questions, and journaling.

As you will see, journaling is integrated into each day even when there's no reading assignment. Journaling is an important part of doing any type of study, it will help you organize your thoughts and write down the specific things that you've found that apply to your own life. It is the best way for you to retain all the ground that you gain during the study as you review your journaling and remember what you've learned about yourself and the healing process.

How to Launch Your Small Group

If you are using this book in a small group setting, this section and the words in **bold** throughout the book are intended for you, the small group leader, and are only in the Leader's guide. The Leader's guide includes the same text as the main book along with additional Leader information.

I highly recommend opening and closing your small group meeting in prayer. It's of great importance to invite God into your small group allowing Him to minister to each individual as needed.

I found it to be a huge help to review the "Intro" section of the chapter that you will be discussing just to refresh everyone on the topic for the week.

You will want to review the questions at the end of each daily section during small group allowing group members to share what they have written. In my experience of using this book in a small group setting, although the reading assignments, journaling, and study questions had been completed in preparation for small group, the discussion time usually caused us to take a few weeks for each chapter. This flexibility allowed everyone the opportunity to share. Please don't let the need to complete this study in a certain number of weeks, stifle the healing process. Be flexible, and enjoy letting people work through the healing process.

Finally, review the "Time for Action" section at the end of the chapter and close in prayer.

The suggested answers, located after some questions, are there to help guide and encourage more discussion topics. Don't forget to share your own answers to the questions.

How to introduce the book to your group at the first meeting.
(Make enough copies of the Confidentiality Agreement

(Appendix A) ahead of time for each of your small group members.)

Open with prayer.

Discuss with your group:

Each individual must have a commitment to healing, and accept your judgment as small group leader. There must be trust and openness within the small group setting. Confidentiality must be maintained. Because of this, we will each sign a Confidentiality Agreement.

Read and have group member's sign the Confidentiality Agreement located in the back of the Leader's Guide.

On the first day of small group, you should give each student their copy of the book and read the Introduction together if desired.

Discuss with your group:

What you as a leader hope to see during small group, for example lots of feedback, commitment to change and growth, honesty, humility, respect, and compassion for each other. Come to small group prepared by having read the assigned chapter. Journaling and completion of the study questions are vital to getting all that you can out of this study.

Ask your small group members the following question:

What do you hope to get out of this study?

Read the Preface on page 1 together.

Discuss:

As you read/heard the Preface, what emotions or feelings did you have?

In what ways can you relate to the situation in the story?

What would you have done or felt if you had been in that same situation?

Share:

As leader, share a bit of your own personal experiences as they relate to the preface of the book. How did you feel? etc.

In order to connect with your students or small group, you need to be willing to be vulnerable. They need to know that you are human, that you have feelings, that you don't necessarily have a "perfect" past. When they see where you have come from and compare that to where you are now, it will give them comfort in sharing and also a hope for their future as they see that you have survived and your life has improved.

Ask if anyone has any questions or would like to share anything further.

Read How to Use This Book together and **Discuss** the following statement:

Healing is a choice; you will get out of this study exactly what you put in to it. As you let yourself connect to the stories of hurts, habits, and hang-ups, search deep within yourself to find areas in your life that you need to heal. You may have never been sexually abused, but have you ever had something happen that shook the foundation of trust and security within your world? You may have never considered suicide, but have you ever felt unwanted, unloved, or abandoned? Have you ever been overwhelmed with hopelessness? As you read, try to relate to the foundational messages within the stories, so that you can get as much out of them as possible.

Explain:

Looking at chapter one's "To Do" list, explain that each day you should read a different section of the chapter that you are working on, you should not read any further than that. Let each days reading assignment soak in, and really dig deep into what that section is talking about. Be sure to read, answer the questions, and journal every day. The sections are split up into days for your convenience. Try to search for something in your life that you can relate to in the section you are reading. Make sure to journal questions, comments, emotions, or anything else that may come to the surface.

Assign the first chapter.

Close in prayer.

Preface

(Please note: This is only the first of many testimonies shared within this book. Please, don't let the following story convince you that this book is only about abuse.)

It is the middle of winter in a small country town. A young 11 year old girl and her 15 year old stepbrother sit on the couch together while watching TV with the rest of their family. They are both covered with a blanket to keep warm; suddenly, the girl feels her stepbrother's hand work its way down between her legs. She is frightened and does not understand. She wants to scream and jump up from the couch and ask him what in the world he is doing, but she is frozen with fear. She wonders why no one else sees what is happening.

Some months later the same girl, now 12, is on her way home from the hardware store with her step dad. The step dad begins to make conversation with the young girl about her sexuality. He begins to talk about seeing her naked and makes mention of wanting to do sexual things to her. She thinks to herself, this could not be real; surely he does not mean this. Her mind starts to consider what her mother has told her to do in such circumstances; so she wonders if this is a test to see if she would obey. Is she supposed to turn off the car, throw the keys out of the window and run as fast as she can like her mom has told her? She doesn't want to believe that he is serious about his sexual advances, but unfortunately he is. This begins the cycle of abuse that would continue for years afterwards.

Hiding the pain of that abuse becomes the norm for her. She begins, at the age of 15, to cover up the pain by abusing alcohol and using various illegal drugs. She doesn't like the hateful and resentful person she has become. She feels lost and trapped within a mere shell of who she once was. Her mother does not know how to deal with her so at the age of 16 she's kicked out of her parent's home and begins life on her own. She is living a reckless life which puts her in unsafe situations that ultimately allow her to be raped by two men, and taken advantage of sexually by others. She doesn't know that her body is precious and that she is valuable for more reasons than to be used for the physical needs of men. She is angry at God for allowing the bad things to happen to her and wonders what value there could be for her life. She feels abandoned, unloved, and forsaken by God.

She said the sinner's prayer at the age of four and remembers the promise of a loving Father in heaven, but she does not "know" Him personally. Then, one evening, at the age of 17 while alone in her apartment, she decides her life is not worth living. Committed to the decision to end it she cries out in quiet desperation to God, "Is this all my life is going to be?!!" To her amazement she hears a response, an internal, but somehow audible voice, a voice that is different from the voice she hears in her thoughts. It is a warm, comforting voice that tells her, "I have better plans for you!" This, she knows beyond a shadow of doubt, is the voice of God and this loving voice has just given her the first glimmer of hope for a life that has felt so worthless and empty. At that moment she begins the journey of healing that God has planned for her. That journey is what this book is about.

"I Have Better Plans for You" has been my life's journey of discovery, as I hope it will become yours.

CHAPTER ONE

TO DO

Week One:

Day One
- ☐ Read the Intro
- ☐ Do the Study Questions
- ☐ Journal

Day Two
- ☐ Read, Why Does God Allow Us to Experience Pain
- ☐ Do the Study Questions
- ☐ Journal

Day Three
- ☐ Read, Allow Yourself to Feel the Pain
- ☐ Do the Study Questions
- ☐ Journal

Day Four
- ☐ Read, Talk about Your Pain
- ☐ Do the Study Questions
- ☐ Journal

Day Five
- ☐ Read, Recognize the Root Cause of Your Pain
- ☐ Do the Study Questions
- ☐ Journal

Day Six
- ☐ Read, Find Hope in the Midst of Your Pain
- ☐ Do the Study Questions
- ☐ Journal

Day Seven
- ☐ Time for Action
- ☐ Journal

Chapter 1
DON'T DENY THE PAIN
Week One Day One

C.S. Lewis said that, "God whispers to us in our pleasures, speaks in our conscience, but shouts in our pain."[1] Without pain, we don't have to rely on anyone else. Pain causes us to seek out help, and to hopefully find the one who is seeking us; God.

Recently, I became aware of a situation that demonstrated what pain can do, and how God can use it. A woman, who was far away from a relationship with Jesus, was given an opportunity to start life over again. She had endured a very painful life and blamed God for it. She didn't understand why He would allow her to suffer like she always had. Rather than run toward Him, she ran from Him. According to her interpretation, any time she would try to draw near to God, bad things would happen so she did her best to stay away. She was blaming God for all the suffering in her life.

Then, one lonely night in 2007 when she felt completely hopeless, and had lost the will to live, she made the decision to take her own life and end her suffering. She proceeded to swallow two bottles of 500mg Acetaminophen, and drank a bottle of cough medicine with codeine, all while drinking alcohol to intensify the effect. Finally, when she felt the time was close, she put a plastic bag over her head in order to seal the deal and hurry death along. God, however, had better plans for her. She was found thirteen long and painful hours later. Miraculously, she was still alive and was rushed to the hospital. Phone calls were made to her family urging them to get to the hospital. They were informed that she was not going to make it; her liver was no longer working like it should. Her only chance for survival was a liver transplant, if one became available. When family arrived at her bedside, they prayed for her, and desperately asked God to heal her. This was the only hope they had, that God would answer their request to heal her and give her another chance at life.

That evening, after the family left the hospital, they found and read the woman's suicide note. In the note, she expressed her pain to her children and told them how sorry she was that she wasn't strong enough. She also mentioned that she would be in a better place "she hoped." The letter revealed just how much pain the woman was dealing with and the family understood the depth of her grief. The woman had always been very good at hiding the truth of her suffering and putting on a "strong front." Her suicide note was a desperate revelation to them all.

The next morning the family returned to the hospital and to their surprise the woman was sitting up in her bed alert and full of color. The relief they felt at seeing their mother's improvement did not hinder the decision they had made to discuss the suicide note with her. During their candid discussion with their mother, one of the children told her that there is a reason God has kept her here, and that she needs to "know" that she would be in a better place, instead of just "hope."

Finally, the amazing news came from the doctor that her liver counts were improving and that he thought it was a miracle. According to her Doctor she had taken enough medicine to kill a horse and several grown men and he couldn't explain her improvement. Her liver had been destroyed, but God was restoring it and within three days, her liver was back to normal and functioning as it should! Glory and Praise be to God! Her family was ecstatic and came to realize that God does answer prayers and they were all radically impacted by witnessing this miracle.

The woman's life was changed dramatically from the experience. She learned that her life has meaning and that God loves her! For the remaining two years of her life she accepted Christ as her Savior and devoted her time to regular attendance and ministry at church. She was baptized in October 2008 and she went to be with the Lord on May 31, 2009, due to emphysema. She lived her final years to the fullest and her family has peace knowing that she "is" in a better place just as she had previously "hoped."

STUDY

---

1) When you are in emotional pain, who do you turn to?

  _____

  friends, teacher, pastor, sibling, God

2) Have you ever been in such a desperate, hopeless, situation that you felt that ending your life would be better?
   If so, describe it...

  _____

  _____

  _____

  _____

DON'T DENY THE PAIN

3) What changed your outlook?

_____

thoughts of family, friends, good memories, fear

4) Are there things in your life that you tend to blame God for?
   What are they, and why do you blame God?

_____

_____

_____

_____

5) Have you ever witnessed a miracle?
   If so, who did you credit for that miracle?

_____

Maybe Doctors, luck etc.

6) Have you ever experienced an answer to prayer?
   If so, what happened?

_____

_____

_____

7) What does an answered prayer reveal to you?

_____

God is right there with you and He is listening, Jer. 33:3

8) Do you recognize miracles and answered prayers as proof of
   the existence of a Father in Heaven who is present and
   participating in your life? Why or Why not?

_____

_____

_____

9) Do you think God always answers prayers in the way that we hope for? Why or Why not?

_____

_____

Review the following section with the group.
Does God always answer prayers? Yes, He does.
Here are four examples of ways that He may answer your prayers.

> 1. He may answer, **"Yes,"** and give you exactly what you ask for.
> 2. He may answer, **"Maybe,"** and give you some of what you ask for, or possibly in a different way.
> 3. He may answer, **"No,"** because He has something better for you or someone else, and His purposes are greater than ours.
> 4. He may answer, **"Not now,"** because His timing is perfect.

No matter how He answers our prayers, we know that, "[...]in all things God works for the good of those who love him, who have been called according to his purpose" (Rom. 8:28).

You may be asking yourself, "How do I know that I am called according to His purpose?" I will break it down for you in just a moment but first I have some questions for you.

Do you hope in your salvation or do you know you are saved?

Webster's definition of *hope*: to desire with expectation of obtainment
Webster's definition of *know*: to be aware of the truth or factuality of: be convinced or certain of

How can we know by being "convinced or certain" of our salvation?

DON'T DENY THE PAIN

"And you, my child, will be called a prophet of the Most High; for you will go on before the Lord to prepare the way for him, to give his people the knowledge of salvation through the forgiveness of their sins" (Luke 1:76-77).

So knowledge of salvation comes through the forgiveness of sins. Well, how do we know our sins are forgiven?

"In him we have redemption through his blood, the forgiveness of sins" (Eph. 1:7).

Because our sins are forgiven through Jesus, we have knowledge of our own salvation through the acceptance of His blood shed on the cross as atonement for our sins.

It is then, through salvation in Christ Jesus, that we become a part of God's family, "[...]In love he predestined us to be adopted as his sons through Jesus Christ" (Eph. 1:4-5).

Since we know we are predestined, we can also know we are called. "And those he predestined, he also called[...]" (Rom. 8:30).

This then takes on the assumption we are called according to His purpose. "[...]by the power of God, who has saved us and called us to a holy life-- not because of anything we have done but because of his own purpose and grace" (2 Tim. 1:8-9).

Because we are called according to His purpose we also know that Romans 8:28, mentioned before, is speaking to us. God is involved and present in our life, He knows our desires and our needs and we can have confidence that He does answer our prayers with either a yes, maybe, no, or not now. Regardless of His answer we know that He is working all things out for the good of those who love Him.

JOURNAL

WHY DOES GOD ALLOW US TO EXPERIENCE PAIN
Week One Day Two

One of the struggles people have when coming to terms with suffering, is the question of why God allows it. They may even wonder where God is at while they are suffering. When I consider these questions I contrast it with being a parent.

I believe that parents, in their love for their child, sometimes have to make the difficult decision to allow their child to fall or make mistakes that can hurt them. In doing so, they realize that their child will learn something from it and hopefully never make the same mistakes again. The parents want their child to know that they love them enough to allow them to go through it, all the while knowing that their child could either choose to turn away from them or hopefully run to them in order to find safety.

When a child learns to walk, sometimes they fall; they may even get hurt as they are learning their new skill. However, the parents are never too far away so when the child does fall they are able to find safety in the arms of their mother and father. If the parents were to keep them from trying, in order to prevent harm from coming to them, they would never learn to walk. The love that the parents have for the child encourages the child to learn from every fall, and to get back up and try again.

It is the same way for God; He does not want to see us

hurt. It is out of His love for us, that He allows us to fall. The fall of course, can represent many painful things, but the important thing to be aware of is that God is right there waiting for us, just like the parents, hoping that we will learn something from the experience, and most importantly, turn to Him and find safety in His arms.

Furthermore, these painful experiences have the ability to teach us compassion which can give us a desire to help other hurting individuals. As a result, we also need to consider pain an important opportunity to learn compassion toward others. So when we look at each painful or difficult situation we need to find a way to learn from it, find compassion toward others, while at the same time drawing closer to our Heavenly Father. These are the reasons I believe God allows us to experience pain and because of this we can know our pain has a purpose.

STUDY

1) Share a time in your life when you have questioned, "Why would God allow this to happen?"

_____

_____

_____

loss of a loved one, a tragic accident, an abusive situation

2) Do you remember a time when your parents allowed you to make a mistake, if so, what did you learn?

_____

_____

_____

_____

3) When it was all said and done, did you get mad at your parents or did you draw closer to them?

_____

4) How did it make you feel?

_____

_____

5) Do tough times cause you to run away or run toward God?

_____

6) How do you run away?

_____

get angry at God, avoid spending time at church or in prayer

7) How do you run toward?

_____

draw closer to God through prayer, bible reading, and worship, reach out to your friends for prayer

8) What purpose have you found for some of the pain you have experienced?

_____

_____

you are able to help other people who are going through something similar by sharing what God has taught you through your situation

JOURNAL

ALLOW YOURSELF TO FEEL THE PAIN
Week One Day Three

All of us have been hurt in some way or other. And each of us deal with those emotions differently. My husband and many others of the same gender, have been taught from a very young age that men do not cry. This, apparently is a common fact among most men. Conversely, for the most part girls have been able to nurture their emotional development. In recent times, however, the roles have changed for girls, who these days will refuse to feel the emotions that go along with everyday life and in turn will begin to show this unfelt emotion through outward behavioral means or through hidden, physical, self-abusive methods.

Regardless of the gender or generation, the battle that rages is one of hidden, unfelt emotion. Thoughts such as, "If I don't feel the pain, it doesn't exist," "Pain cannot control me," "No one needs to know I'm hurting," "Admitting that I'm hurting means that I'm weak," or "People will think I just want sympathy," these are all lies of the enemy. The truth is, as you may have heard before, "you can't heal it if you don't feel it." And while we are on this topic, I want you to consider something else that I have heard many times over the years, "hurt people; hurt people." You may not even realize that you could be hurting others, but when you hide your pain it will show up in your attitudes and behaviors toward other people.

Therefore, one of the first steps to dealing with the pain of have trained yourself not to. You have no doubt become numb to emotion. You may have yourself convinced there is so much buried pain that if you begin to feel it the floodgates are going to burst. I expect you think all of those tears and emotions that have been put off are going to spill out in one big wave that will flood your life and make it unbearable. You are probably saying to yourself, "I have been hurt enough so why encourage more of it?" That can be very frightening and it is understandable that you would try to avoid it.

The pain of these past emotions are going to seem impossible to handle, I understand that. But I have a couple of promises for you that come from God's Word, "[you], can do everything through Him who gives [you] strength" (Phil. 4:13). "In this world you will have trouble. But take heart! I have overcome the world" (Jn. 16:33). God will give you the strength to handle the pain. He will walk you through it step by step. He will help you overcome because He has already overcome the world! Just ask Him to help you begin the process.

I think by now you've probably learned that buried pain never stays buried. I have seen pain expressed in various ways; such as, drug abuse, sexual promiscuity, cutting, and eating disorders. However, the most extreme that I am aware of, has to be the method of burning.

"Cindy," as I will call her, had repressed her emotions so deeply that in order to cope with her buried pain she would burn herself. She would let the head of a lighter get red hot and then press it in to her bare shoulder until it cooled down. This act would cause a burn so severe that she would have "v" shaped, ¼ inch deep holes in her skin. This became a regular outlet for her pain, which has left her with multiple raised scars.

When I challenged Cindy to begin the process of allowing herself to finally feel her pain without the use of a lighter, she expressed her fear of not being able to handle it. I myself am amazed that she thought the burning was easier to handle than the emotional pain itself. What became apparent to me is that her buried pain must have been much more extensive than the pain that she inflicted upon herself with the lighter. However, once Cindy started to work through the pain in her life, she realized that God was not going to make her deal with it all at once. He was taking her through it layer by layer. Trust Him to do the same with you as you begin to uncover your buried pain.

Whatever unhealthy method you have been using to bury, cover up, or avoid dealing with your pain, it is extremely important for you to make the decision to stop that behavior right now. It is only causing more pain and destruction, and it is actually prolonging the healing process. Consider the physical scaring that Cindy caused herself by trying to hide her pain. Maybe, the scars you are causing yourself are not as visible, but you are certainly causing yourself more harm by not dealing with your pain in a healthy way.

It is so crucial for you to understand that you cannot deal with the pain if you are still doing everything in your power to avoid it! The time has come for you to face the pain and begin to cope with it in a healthy way, and since you are reading this book the chances are you realize that already. You are making the right choice, be confident of that!

STUDY

---

1) How do you deal with pain?

_____

_____

maybe try to hide it, ignore it, pretend it doesn't exist, or do you face it, talk about it etc.

DON'T DENY THE PAIN

2) What have you been using/doing to bury or cover up your
   pain?

   _____

   _____

3) When you ignore your pain, in what ways does it reveal itself?

   _____

   _____

   _____

   anger toward others, drug/alcohol abuse, or self mutilation

4) What can you do in order to begin dealing with your pain in a
   healthy way?

   _____

   _____

   **talk about it, journal it, cry (it's ok to cry), pray and tell God,
   don't be afraid to tell God that you are angry**

5) What behavior(s) do you need to stop doing that is causing
   more harm than good?

   _____

   _____

   _____

   _____

   **Ask the small group to commit to stopping this behavior, or
   begin to pray that God would give them the desire and ability to
   stop.**

JOURNAL

_____

_____
_____
_____
_____
_____
_____
_____
_____
_____
_____
_____
_____
_____
_____
_____
_____
_____
_____
_____
_____
_____
_____
_____
_____
_____
_____
_____
_____
_____
_____
_____

DON'T DENY THE PAIN

TALK ABOUT YOUR PAIN
Week One Day Four

   The next step in the healing process, is learning to talk about your pain. Talk to God about the pain you are feeling, He knows you are hurting and wants to help you. "Record my lament; list my tears on your scroll are they not in your record?" (Ps. 56:8). This verse suggests that God has kept a record of your tears. He knows how many tears you have shed, He is not unaware of your pain. God is so concerned about you that He actually keeps a record of your suffering.

   Ask God to help you heal and believe that He will answer your prayers. Psalm 6:8 says, "Away from me, all you who do evil, for the Lord has heard my weeping. The Lord has heard my cry for mercy; the Lord accepts my prayer." Be honest with Him, in doing this it will help you talk to others about it.

   Once you begin to talk to God about your pain, you will also need to find a safe person to share your pain with. According to Dr. Henry Cloud and Dr. John Townsend who wrote the book *Safe People*[2], a safe person is someone who, "draws us closer to God," "draws us closer to others," and "helps us become the real person God created us to be." You need someone who you can share your true feelings with and not have to worry about whether they will judge you or talk about you. Can they keep the things that you share with them between just you and them?

While we are on this topic, I personally tell my small group girls that I will keep everything between just them and I, unless it is a safety issue, their safety is my number one concern. I also promise that if there is anything that needs to be shared with another person that they will not be alone, that I will be with them through the entire process. I request their acceptance of this before they ever begin to share anything. You should be willing to give the same permission to your safe person. Recognize that it is for your own safety. If they feel it is necessary to reach out to someone else in order to help you, trust them to make the right decision for you.

Another aspect of a safe person is someone who will help you to grow. Will they hold you accountable, and can you accept the accountability they give you? A safe person will always challenge you in love without condemnation or confrontation and also direct you back to the scriptures to seek God for help. They will be able to listen without always trying to fix you or your problems because sometimes you just need someone who's willing to listen. They need to encourage and uplift you even while they are correcting you and you should be comfortable receiving correction from this person without getting angry or defensive with them. They will also share with you their own struggles and weaknesses. In sharing they will show that they are willing to be open and honest with you and that they have no pretense. They will not be self-serving but will genuinely be there for you. You need to be willing to be vulnerable, and to open up and share with this person, so it should be someone you can trust. This person could be your Pastor, Counselor or even a close friend to begin with. I would certainly recommend seeking professional counseling in any case.

The point is you need to expose your secrets to the light by talking about them. Secrets give Satan power over your thoughts. When you expose your secrets, Satan loses the power to use them against you through thoughts of shame, guilt, and bitterness, and his lies lose their sting. Stop avoiding the feelings. When you avoid talking about strong feelings it doesn't make them go away, in fact, they become more pronounced in our attempts to live as though they don't exist. Do not let the past control your future any longer, confront those feelings and begin talking about your pain.

STUDY

Discuss prayer, how to etc. Prayer is talking to God just like He was right there in the room with you.
During your daily quiet time, take time to pray and ask God to help you heal from your pain, and rebuke Satan's attempts to harm you. This may be difficult or awkward for you if you are not used to praying, but it is a vital step. Be humble and surrender to God asking Him for help. It is important to talk to God about your struggles.
Take some time right now to pray as mentioned above, asking God to heal you, and being honest with Him about your pain.

1) How do you feel after that time of prayer?

_____

possibly refreshed, like a weight has been lifted, encouraged

2) Do you have anyone in your life that you consider a safe person? What is it about them that makes them safe?

_____
_____
_____

Remind the group to...
Find a safe person if you do not have one already. Besides learning to talk to God, you will also need to learn to talk to a

safe person about your struggles. We were not meant to do life alone. We were made for community and fellowship.

3) How does it make you feel when you are able to talk about your pain?

_____

_____

_____

_____

4) What impact do you think it will have on you and your daily life when you are able to talk about your story and share your pain?

_____

_____

_____

_____

JOURNAL

_____

_____
_____
_____
_____
_____
_____
_____
_____
_____
_____
_____
_____
_____
_____
_____
_____
_____
_____
_____
_____
_____
_____
_____
_____
_____
_____
_____
_____
_____
_____
_____
_____

DON'T DENY THE PAIN

RECOGNIZE THE ROOT CAUSE
OF YOUR PAIN
Week One Day Five

One very important component to the healing process is learning to recognize the root cause of your pain and suffering. God is not the cause of your pain; therefore you need to put blame where blame is due.

God created us as emotional beings, with the ability to feel. What a wonderful gift He has blessed us with. We can laugh, cry, experience joy; even anger is a God given emotion. He has also supplied us with a system of sensory nerves that allow us to feel physical pain. Our sensory nerves allow us to feel what I would call, "good pain." That is, pain that warns you not to touch something hot, or allows you to recognize when you have been injured. Good pain has existed since creation, and it serves a God given purpose. Pain is a natural part of life, but I feel that pain, as we experience it today, was not in God's original design.

I am sure you would agree with me when I say, not all pain is good and not all pain has a God given purpose; although I do believe God can give our pain a purpose. The pain of disease, death, emotional pain, and overall suffering is the direct result of the fall of man. God said to Adam after he ate the forbidden fruit, "Cursed is the ground because of you; through painful toil you will eat of it all the days of your life" (Gen. 3:17). God also told Eve that He would "greatly increase her pains in childbirth" (Gen. 3:16). Adam and Eve, after being deceived by the devil, ushered sin into this once perfect world through their one act of disobedience. The bible says, "The thief comes only to steal, kill, and destroy; I have come that they may have life, and have it to the full" (Jn. 10:10). Sin and the work of the devil are the root causes of pain and suffering in the world today, and because of free will we are subject to the sins of others as well as our own sinful choices. Sin changed the way we experience pain.

Back to the subject of putting blame where blame is due, I want to share another very important lesson that I have learned. For many years I unintentionally punished my husband for what other men had done to me, mainly as a result of the abuse from my step father and the rape that I had still not even admitted to. This unfair treatment toward my husband was a subconscious result of how I was hurting deep inside.

My lack of knowledge and understanding of what I was actually doing, kept me from recognizing that I had equated my husband to the pain and abuse inflicted upon me by other men. He, simply by being a man in a position of importance in my life, took on the unspoken title of abuser.

In one moment of brilliantly swift observation on my husband's part, he made the comment, through tears of frustration, "I am not your father! I did not do this to you; I did not hurt you!" It was in that moment of revelation that I realized how much pain I had been causing my husband. I was making him bear the punishment I was unable to inflict on the ones who hurt me. In his moment of vulnerability, he revealed the truth to me.

I needed to stop treating my husband as someone unsafe, and untrustworthy. I needed to recognize that not all men will hurt me; some actually want to love me fully and unconditionally. I needed to learn how to allow him to love me.

If you are punishing someone for another person's sin, you

need to recognize what you are doing and put a stop to it. Stop causing undue harm to the innocent person who truly loves you, and allow yourself to accept their love. You must believe that you deserve to be loved and learn that you can return that love without fear.

The healing process may seem overwhelming to you at this point but don't get discouraged! God can give you a purpose for the pain that you have experienced and He can allow you the opportunity to finally become victorious instead of being a victim.

Once you find victory from the pain of your past it will be like slapping the face of the enemy, what the enemy intended to destroy us our Heavenly Father can use for His good purpose. Joseph said to his brothers, "you intended to harm me, but God intended it for good to accomplish what is now being done, the saving of many lives" (Gen. 50:20). Do not allow your pain to be without purpose!

STUDY

1) What or who causes pain?

   sin, satan, our own free and the free will of others

2) Pain, the way we experience it today, was not in God's "perfect" plan, but who created pain? Read Gen. 3:16-17

   God created all things, even pain

3) Why do you think God created pain?

DON'T DENY THE PAIN

4) Why does God allow pain and suffering?

_____

_____

5) Who have you been blaming for your pain that you shouldn't have been?

_____

_____

God, yourself, your children, spouse, parents, siblings etc.

6) In what ways are you punishing the undeserved?

_____

**Remember hurt people, hurt people: Are they lashing out in anger for no reason, being disrespectful, treating them
the way they wish that they could treat the one who hurt them?**

7) In what ways are you preventing people from loving you?

_____

_____

avoidance, being so mean to people that they want to stay away, refusing any kindness from them

8) How can you learn to accept love?

_____

allow people to show you kindness, or spend quality time with you, be kind in return, realize that not everyone will hurt you

9) There is a purpose for your pain, how can you discover what that purpose is?

_____

_____

draw closer to God, ask Him to reveal His purpose for your pain

JOURNAL

_____

_____
_____
_____
_____
_____
_____
_____
_____
_____
_____
_____
_____
_____
_____
_____
_____
_____
_____
_____
_____
_____
_____
_____
_____
_____
_____
_____
_____
_____
_____

DON'T DENY THE PAIN

FIND HOPE IN THE MIDST
OF YOUR PAIN
Week One Day Six

When you suffer, one of the hardest things to possess is a sense of hope. From what I've witnessed over the years, it is much more common to believe that things can never get any better, or that life just isn't working for you. It can feel like there is never going to be a light at the end of the tunnel. That is why I believe that hope is a vital component of healing, hope in God, hope in health, hope in a future, a hope that life can hold more meaning than it has in the past.

You may feel that you do not matter, that you were just a mistake, or that your life has no purpose. You may actually hear words like, "you're worthless," "you were an accident," or "you are nothing but trouble," etc. On the other hand, a sibling or parent may not have to say those words exactly; they could simply imply that you are not important, or that you seem to be more trouble than you are worth.

In my personal experience, all I needed to hear was the story of my moms past to know that I was not planned by my parents. Unfortunately, like many others, I did not hear stories of how they waited to hear the news of a child on the way, or how my mother surprised my father with the wonderful news in some creative way.

My mother was 16 years old when she became pregnant with her first child and then had three children by the time she was 21. She was stressed, overworked, and had a troubled and abusive relationship with my father. She was unaware of the impact that her life story had on me. I felt like more of a burden to her, or at the least, a constant reminder of the terrible mental and physical abuse she suffered at the hands of my father, especially since she would tell me that I looked so much like him.

There were many things that my mother said over the years that made me feel like I was unwanted and a burden. In fact, my mom told me many times that she almost put me up for adoption but then she decided not to.

In my case, the feeling of being unwanted was more of a self imposed impression based upon my experiences rather than a purposeful attempt by my mother to make me feel that way.

Regardless of the situation, thoughts of worthlessness can negate any sense of hope that you may have.

Can I boldly ask, what has made you feel worthless, without purpose, or like an accident? Or better yet, what has made you lose hope?

Let's contrast these feelings with what Gods word says about you. "Before I formed you in the womb I knew you, before you were born I set you apart" (Jer. 1:5). What a revelation! God formed you in the womb which takes planning, and planning takes time. God took the time to think you through. He knew you before your mother carried you in her womb! He knew exactly what color hair you would have, He knew the precise time of your birth before it came to pass, and He knows exactly when you will take your final breath (Ps. 139:15-16).

Not only did He plan you, but God also has a plan for your life. "For I know the plans I have for you, declares the Lord, plans to prosper you and not to harm you, plans to give you hope and a future" (Jer. 29:11). Does that give you hope knowing that your life has purpose and that it has value in God's eyes? I envision God as a sculptor, tenderly molding the clay that forms you and choosing every aspect of who you are with tender, loving attention. Contrary to what you've believed in the past, you are not a mistake; you were planned and designed by God. There is most certainly hope in that knowledge. You were planned and designed for a purpose!

You can also find hope in the eternal future. "Never again will they hunger, never again will they thirst. The sun will not beat upon them, nor any scorching heat. For the Lamb at the center of the throne will be their shepherd; he will lead them to springs of living water. And God will wipe away every tear from their eyes" (Rev. 7:10). Your future, in heaven, will be void of tears and pain. No longer will you be subjected to the sin and suffering that the world is saturated with. My prayer for you is that you find hope in the promise of eternity in heaven with your Heavenly Father. "There is surely a future hope for you, and your hope will not be cut off" (Pr. 23:18).

Remember, God has better plans for you, cling to that promise and let that be the source of your hope as it has been mine. Live your life with purpose!

STUDY

_____

1) Were you planned or an accident? Who says?

_____

_____

your parents may have said you were an accident, but the bible tells a different story

2) What is hope? (we read the definition on day 1)

_____

DON'T DENY THE PAIN

3) Where do you find hope? What do you hope for?

_____

in your future, in God's plans for your life, in your potential etc.

4) Do you believe that there is a purpose for everything? _____

5) What about you, do you have a purpose?

_____

   Review the following verses
   Read Isaiah 64:8, and Jer. 1:5
   So you are not an accident, God planned you, tenderly
   formed you, and gave you life.

6) Why would God have taken the time to create you? Read Jer.
   29:11-13

_____

He wants us to seek Him and He has plans to give us a hope and a future. Yes, He has plans for your future!

7) What purpose do you think He has for you and your future?

_____

_____

_____

8) What are some ways that you can find out what that purpose
   is?

_____

_____

_____

ask the one who created you, "God what is my purpose in life?" Start to serve in an area of ministry that you feel a passion for, or use the talents that He has given you

9) Do you think that God will answer you if you ask Him to reveal His purpose for you? Read Jer. 33:3

_____

Why wouldn't He? He created you with a purpose and you can bet He wants that purpose fulfilled!

Is there hope in that knowledge? Yes!

Don't waste time wondering if there is hope for your life, grab hold of the hope and knowledge that God planned you and has plans for you. Live your life with purpose!

JOURNAL

_____

_____
_____
_____
_____
_____
_____
_____
_____
_____
_____
_____
_____
_____
_____
_____
_____
_____
_____
_____
_____
_____
_____
_____
_____
_____
_____
_____
_____
_____
_____
_____
_____
_____

DON'T DENY THE PAIN

TIME FOR ACTION
Week One Day Seven

☐ I commit to begin facing the pain of my past
☐ I commit to Pray and ask God to help me heal from the pain of my past
☐ I commit to share my pain with others and to seek counseling
☐ I commit to put blame where blame is due
☐ I commit to find hope in the midst of my suffering

On the next page, write about the areas of your life that have caused you pain, talk about how you are dealing with the pain, or make a plan for beginning to work through the pain.

JOURNAL

CHAPTER
TWO

TO DO

Week Two:

Day One
- ☐ Read the Intro
- ☐ Do the Study Questions
- ☐ Journal

Day Two
- ☐ Read, Confess Your Sins to God
- ☐ Do the Study Questions
- ☐ Journal

Day Three
- ☐ Read, Ask God to Reveal Unknown Sins
- ☐ Do the Study Questions
- ☐ Journal

Day Four
- ☐ Read, Confess Habitual Sins to a Spiritual Mentor
- ☐ Do the Study Questions
- ☐ Journal

Day Five
- ☐ Read, Confess Sins Perpetrated to Others
- ☐ Do the Study Questions
- ☐ Journal

Day Six
- ☐ Journal

Day Seven
- ☐ Time for Action
- ☐ Journal

Chapter 2
CONFESSION AND REPENTANCE

Week Two Day One

Confession and repentance are pivotal to a saving relationship with Christ Jesus. I had already confessed my sins to God and repented; I knew that they were forgiven. However, I also knew, through the work of the Holy Spirit in my life, that I had secrets God wanted me to confess to my husband. The guilt of those secrets weighed so heavily on me. Those secrets had become part of a wall that I had built between God and myself which kept me from going deeper in my relationship with Him and also kept me from being truly close to my husband.

I desired to break down that wall, and draw closer to God and my husband, but I was so afraid of the consequences. I was afraid of losing my husband. I began to pray that God would show me the right timing and give me the strength to do what I knew I must. I needed to explain to my husband that I had been raped by two men when I was 17. He knew about the abuse from my childhood but he did not know about the rape. Not only did I have to admit to being raped, but there were a few times where under aged drinking had left me alone with men who took advantage of me sexually. Since I began at an early age to believe I was obligated to fulfill the needs of men, I never learned to say no. I assumed that I must have done something to lead these men on and so I felt pressured to do what they wanted.

While I was going through these violations I would disconnect myself from the situation to the point of feeling like a shell of a person; I was no longer there emotionally. What made it worse is that I felt responsible for the things that happened to me. I took the blame because I had allowed myself to be put in these situations, so shame and guilt were added to the mix of emotional turmoil. The thought that this was my fault was, of course, a lie of the enemy. Yes, I could have been more responsible for my own safety, but I did not cause these things to happen. I could not control what had been done to me in any of these circumstances. Nevertheless, shame and guilt were making it difficult for me to confess.

It was tearing me up inside knowing that I had been with other men and that my husband did not know about them. It was going to be difficult for both of us, but the wall, built by all these secrets, needed to be destroyed completely.

The next step was to pray and wait for God's timing. I asked God for strength, and the right words to say. I prayed that God would prepare my husband's heart to hear the truth and for my husband to forgive me. I had to believe that God was going to answer those prayers.

I knew it was time when the weight of the burden became too much for me to bear. It was at that time that I began to tell the truth and confess to my husband all that had happened. I asked him to forgive me for not telling him sooner and I praise God that, in time, he was able to. It was painful for him to hear the truth, and it just about killed me to have to tell him, but since he has forgiven me we have shared an even deeper relationship than ever before knowing that there are no more secrets between us.

With Gods help, I was freed from the secrets of the past and the wall was finally destroyed! At last! I was able to let God and my husband into that deeper area of my heart.

STUDY

Note: In the following questions, we are talking about walls that prevent healthy relationships; we are not talking about healthy boundaries. Healthy boundaries are good to have and we will be discussing those soon.

1) Who are you unable to be close to because of walls that you have put up?

_____

_____

_____

God, family, friends

2) What are those walls built from, or made of?

_____

_____

_____

secrets, sins, guilt, shame

3) Have you been heavily burdened by these things? In what ways does it affect you?

_____

_____

_____

unable to feel safe in relationships, inability to trust

4) What are the possible consequences if you share these hidden things that make up the walls?

_____

_____

_____

_____

5) What are the possible benefits?

_____

_____

_____

healing, forgiveness, acceptance, deeper love, restoration of trust

6) What are the fears that keep you from sharing?

_____

_____

7) Do you think the benefits outweigh the consequences? Why?

_____

_____

8) How can you destroy these dividing walls built by secrets?

_____

confession, honesty, forgiveness, and repentance

9) What things are you blaming yourself for that you had no control of?

_____

_____

_____

remind everyone: you cannot control what other people do, stop punishing yourself for things that are out of your control

JOURNAL

CONFESS YOUR SINS TO GOD
Week Two Day Two

God is so patient in waiting for us, He does not push, and He will not invade. God will only enter into the areas of our life that we allow Him to. Because of that, before we begin this next step, I feel that it is important to make sure that salvation has taken place in your life.

Why do you need salvation? "[...]for all have sinned and fall short of the glory of God" (Rom. 3:23). This verse says it all, we have all sinned; none of us are perfect. I've known people who've said that they needed to get their life straight before they will make the decision to accept Christ as their Savior. Or they needed to break such and such habit before they commit. My comment to them is always the same, "You cannot even begin to get your life straight without the work of the Holy Spirit, and you will never be perfect, none of us will."

God does not say in His word, come to me, all you who are perfect and don't need a Savior. His word says, "Come to me, all you who are weary and burdened, and I will give you rest" (Matt. 11:28). Sin is what makes the soul "weary and burdened" and as we know from the previous verse, all have sinned. So what do you do about it? "It's as easy as A, B, and C," Admit, Believe, and Commit.

The first step is to Admit that you are a sinner. "If we claim to be without sin, we deceive ourselves and truth is not in us" (1 Jn. 1:8). Have you ever told a lie (even the smallest one), stolen anything (no matter the size), or used God's name in vain? That is just three of the sins described in the Ten Commandments; and if you were judged right now in the court of law based on the Ten Commandments would you be guilty or innocent? Of course, you would be guilty and would deserve punishment.[1] "Whoever shall keep the whole law, and yet stumble in one point, he is guilty of all" (Js. 2:10). But thankfully, someone has paid the penalty for you already and that was Christ Jesus on the cross. "He himself bore our sins in His body on the tree, that we might die to sin and live to righteousness" (1 Pet. 2:24).

Second, you need to Believe that Christ died to save you from your sins, "For God so loved the world, that He gave His only Son, that whoever believes in Him should not perish but have eternal life. For God did not send His Son into the world to condemn the world, but in order that the world might be saved through Him" (Jn. 3:16-17).

Third, you Commit to live your life for Him. That means that you commit to live your life according to the Word of God and turn away from your sins (Ps. 119:9-11), that you build a relationship with your Heavenly Father by reading His Word (Dt. 8:3), and spending time with Him in prayer (Phil. 4:6; Col. 4:2), that you become a part of the Body of Christ by getting connected to a church or a fellowship of believers (Eph. 4:25), and finally that you begin to serve Him using the gifts that the Holy Spirit has imparted to you (1 Pet. 4:10).

If you are ready to make this eternal decision repeat this prayer, or feel free to use your own words.

Heavenly Father, I admit that I am a sinner and that I have lived my life according to my will and not yours. I believe that you sent your Son to die on the cross for my sins and that my sins are forgiven. I accept your forgiveness and believe that Jesus rose again from the dead and because He lives I will also live eternally with Him in heaven. I commit to turn from my sins and live my life according to your will. I ask you Father to come into my life and I ask that you would fill me with your Holy Spirit. In Jesus' name, Amen.

If you have just prayed that prayer for the first time, I would encourage you to tell someone about it as soon as possible and then make plans to be baptized (Acts 2:38).

Let me be the first to welcome you and congratulate you on making the choice to join the Family of God!

Now, we've all heard it said that, "Confession is good for the soul." Where did that statement originate from? How do we know that confession is good for the soul? We can base our answer on what the scriptures say about confession. "If we confess our sins, He is faithful and just and will forgive us our sins and purify us from all unrighteousness" (1Jn. 1:9).

From the time that sin entered the world we have been in need of cleansing through confession. It should be a part of our daily time with God; confession is not a one time event that takes place at salvation, it should be a daily reflection of our struggles to live a Godly life. When we confess our sins to God we should also ask God to help us never sin in that way again. We are to continuously strive to live, like Christ, a sinless life.

Although, it is impossible for us to be perfect like Christ, we can, through salvation, confession, and repentance, be "white as snow" in Gods eyes (Isa. 1:18). The point is to confess and turn away (repent) from the sins we have committed. Salvation is a one time event, but confession and repentance should be a daily result of our desire to live the life that gives God glory; a life that strives to be like Christ.

God already knows what we have done, we will not surprise Him. In *God's Remedy for Rejection* Derek Prince says, "You can always open up to the Lord and tell Him all your hidden secrets.

CONFESSION AND REPENTANCE

You never embarrass or shock Him, and He will never reject you. You can tell Him the worst thing that ever happened to you, and He will respond, I knew it all along, and I still love you."[2] Don't let the fear of disappointing God keep you from confession and repentance.

STUDY

1) Are there areas of your life that you need to allow God into through confession? What are they?

2) What does it mean to confess your sins to God?

to acknowledge your sins to God, to admit you've sinned, you should try to be specific if possible

3) Is confession a one time event that only happens at salvation?

no, it should be a daily reflection of our weaknesses, and an opportunity to ask God for forgiveness and strength to defeat the sins in our life, it should keep us humble

4) When should you confess?

any time that you recognize sin in your life, maybe even several times a day

5) What is keeping you from confessing?

_____

_____

shame, guilt, fear

6) Do you think that you will ever shock God by your confessions?

_____

God is omniscient (all knowing) He already knows what you have done, you will not shock Him

7) Do you fear rejection from God? _____

8) Where else in your life have you felt rejection?

_____

_____

_____

_____

9) Do you think it's realistic to fear that God will reject you? Why, or why not?

_____

_____

_____

_____

Psalm 94:14 says, "For the Lord will not reject his people; he will never forsake his inheritance."
Memorize this verse, it will help you to recall this promise when you fear rejection or if you ever feel rejected.

JOURNAL

ASK GOD TO REVEAL UNKNOWN SINS
Week Two Day Three

We can have sin in our life that we are not even aware of so we need to ask God to make us more aware of the unknown sin in our lives. God will reveal our sins to us in order that we can ask for forgiveness and repent of them. He desires us to grow to be more like Christ. The more time you spend reading His Word and quiet time in prayer, the more you will learn to hear from God. God will in turn use the Holy Spirit, His Word, and sometimes other people to reveal sin in our lives. Out of obedience to Him, we then need to confess and repent of those sins.

Earlier on in my life when I had chosen to use drugs to cover up my pain, I was unaware of the fact that I had created my own god. Speed had become my god; it was the one I turned to when I suffered and the one I relied on. When I started to remember the past, I took speed. When I was depressed, I took speed. When I was mad, I took speed. At a time in my life when I should have been relying on the one true God, I turned to something that was destructive and less than powerful. The One who could truly help me was just waiting for me to recognize that I needed Him and only Him, not the false god that I had been seeking relief from.

I had been taking speed since I was 15. I had become so reliant on the drug that I didn't go a day without it and I used it throughout the day. (Just imagine what life would be like if everyone actually sought God's help throughout the day, every day!!) I did not realize the extent of my sin, but as I began to develop my relationship with God, He alone was able to reveal the position that I had given to the false god in my life, a position that only the true God should have. God's law says, "You shall have no other gods before me" (Ex. 20:3). I had broken the first of the Ten Commandments, and had not even been aware of it! Don't get me wrong, I knew that I should not be using drugs, but I didn't realize that in doing so, I had replaced God's position in my life with the drugs themselves. Oh, how I was humbled when I realized that! Once God revealed this sin to me, I turned from it right away. With His help, I quit taking speed that instant, at the age of 18. I am so thankful that God opened my eyes to this sin and helped take the addiction away from me.

This was the first of many sins in my life that God has revealed to me, and He is still faithful in revealing sins that I have allowed in my life on a day to day basis. He will do the same for you if you are attentive and listening to the Holy Spirit. God has many things that He wants to do with your life and your obedience to Him, through the confession and repentance of the sins revealed to you, will deepen your relationship with the Father, allowing Him to fulfill His purpose in your life.

STUDY

---

1) How can God reveal unknown sin in your life?

_____

_____

the bible, through the holy spirit, your conscience, prayer, and through friends or family etc.

2) What should you do when you discover sin in your life?

confess, repent, ask forgiveness, ask God to help you stop the behavior

Take time to pray right now and ask God to reveal areas in your life where there are unknown sins.
Have everyone find a quiet place to pray. After several minutes call them back into the group.

3) What sins have been revealed to you during your time of prayer?

_____

_____

_____

_____

_____

4) How can you break free from this sinful habit or behavior?

_____

_____

_____

_____

JOURNAL

CONFESS HABITUAL SINS TO A SPIRITUAL MENTOR
Week Two Day Four

You are probably aware of habitual sins in your life, especially if you have been using them in your efforts to cover up the pain as we talked about earlier. Habitual sins are those things that you have struggled to stop doing but have been unsuccessful as of yet. It could be excessive drinking, drugs, smoking, cutting, burning, pornography, eating disorders, gambling, etc. The point is it's an unhealthy coping mechanism, and something that you frequently revert to.

In order to break free from your habitual sins, it's crucial for you to find someone who can hold you accountable if you give in to the temptation to do it again. In other words you need a spiritual mentor, some people call them accountability partners; this could be the same person that we discussed in chapter one as the safe person.

The spiritual mentor should be someone that you feel comfortable with, someone you feel that you can be honest with and that you can trust. They need to be strong in their walk with the Lord and they need to be bold enough to speak into your life and hold you accountable. You can't break free from habitual sins if you are not willing to be held accountable for them.

It's very important for you to ask yourself, "Am I ready to be held accountable? Am I ready to be set free?" If you are still in bondage and cannot say yes to these questions, ask someone to pray over you to break that bondage from you. You can also ask God to give you the desire to be held accountable and break this cycle of sin. It is vital that you want to be set free from it; if you don't, then you will have no will power to fight the temptations that will come your way.

Be willing to be open and honest with your spiritual mentor at all times. Don't be ashamed, we have all had our own habitual sins. Your mentor should be someone that you know you will feel comfortable enough to honestly share your struggles with, and your victories. This person will be someone that will celebrate with you when you have victories, cry with you when you feel like crying and be strong for you when you are weak. When you are struggling with temptation you need to be able to call them for immediate support. You may desire to be free from these habitual sins, but temptations can be so strong and your ability to fight them can sometimes fall short. Your mentor can strengthen you during those times of weakness.

Most importantly, you need to trust your mentor if they want to bring in extra support from someone else, even a professional, especially if your habitual sin is something that is putting you at risk. Realize that your spiritual mentor is showing good judgment and cares enough about you to recognize that they are not equipped to help you and that they need to bring in someone with more knowledge in this area. If you have truly committed to the idea of breaking free from the bondage of habitual sin, you need to be willing to surrender yourself to the better judgment of your spiritual mentor.

Although God should always be your number one support, He has also put people in your path to speak into your life and help you to grow. Be open and honest to yourself, God, and your spiritual mentor. Confess your habitual sins to your mentor. You should understand that this type of confession is not necessary for forgiveness because your sins are forgiven once you accept Christ as your Savior. However, confession to your mentor is extremely important for your accountability and healing. "Therefore confess your sins to each other and pray for each other so that you may be healed[...]" (James 5:16). Being completely honest is the only way to break free. No more hiding behind addictive behaviors!

The habitual sin you are trying to break free from may actually be your way of coping with your pain. Because of this, you will also need to find a healthy coping mechanism to replace it with. Your mentor or counselor can help you find some that will work for you, but in the meantime, here are some of my suggestions. When you start to feel the need or temptation to resort to your unhealthy coping mechanism, try taking a walk to unwind while praying or listening to worship music. Or find a quiet place to pray, listen to worship music and read your Bible. You can also try talking through the temptation with your mentor or someone else. Another alternative could be writing in your journal or doing something creative, like drawing or painting. These are just a few ideas to help you as you begin finding a healthy replacement for the habitual sin in your life.

Breaking free from these habitual sins will be easier when you confess them to your mentor and find a healthy replacement. You CAN be set free!

STUDY

1) Do you need to confess your sins to another person in order for them to be forgiven by God?

No! Your sins were forgiven when you accepted Christ.

2) Why is it important to confess your sinful habits to a mentor?

_____

**for accountability, support, and encouragement while breaking
free from them**

Confession to a mentor can help by holding you accountable as
you begin turning away from those sins. Habitual sins are hard
to break on your own; you will have a better chance with a
spiritual mentor.

3) List the habitual sins that you need to break free from.

_____

_____

_____

4) Are these sinful habits/behaviors helping you or causing you
   more harm? _____

5) Are they harming you physically, emotionally, or spiritually?

_____

6) What can you do to break free from these habits?

_____

_____

_____

**confess, and make the decision for yourself to stop this behavior,
be willing to be held accountable**

Be committed to your healing, and trust your spiritual
mentor!

7) What healthy replacements can you make for the unhealthy
   things you have been using to cope?

_____

_____

_____

JOURNAL

CONFESS SINS PERPETRATED TO OTHERS
Week Two Day Five

We have all hurt someone else at some point, possibly several times over our lifetime. Consider the fact that everything we say or do affects someone else either negatively or positively. So even though we may not realize it, we have most certainly caused harm to someone else.

Obviously, it is impossible to go to each and every person that you have hurt and confess to them. That is unnecessary. However, I am sure that there are certain people who it has weighed heavy on your heart how you have sinned against them. If you've already confessed these sins to God, you need to ask God to confirm in you those people you should confess to directly. Right now you may be carrying a heavy burden over what you have done, and confessing it to them and then asking them for forgiveness will remove the weight of that burden once and for all, possibly for each of you. The person you confess to may really need this confession from you in order to find healing for themselves.

As I shared with you at the beginning of this chapter, many years ago, still early on in my relationship with my future husband, I made the mistake of not guarding my body and refusing to admit to myself and to him that I was raped. Keeping this information from him was wrong, and it was a mistake that haunted me for many years and kept me from being able to feel safe in my marriage. I always felt as if our marriage was teetering on a cliff and at any moment it could fall. I was carrying the burden of these hidden truths and I knew that I needed to confess it all to him. The burden became so strong that I knew I had no other choice. The risk was clear, I could lose my marriage and destroy our family. But the idea of never being able to feel safe and secure in my marriage and free from the burden of guilt and shame was too much to bear. I had to confess.

Ultimately, the risk of confessing these things to my husband was worth it for our situation. I would have to say that I am grateful to have a forgiving husband who was able to see beyond the past and move on to the future free from the secrets between us. I know this is not the case for everyone. That is why it is important for you to seek God and pray for the individual that you will be confessing to. Ask God to prepare them for the truth and pray that they would be willing to forgive you. Be very sure that your confession to the individual is what God is calling you to do. If the confession is better left between you and God then leave it that way, and be confident with your decision.

STUDY

1) When you think about the people you have hurt in the past, who comes to your mind?

_____

_____

2) In what ways have you caused them harm?

_____

_____

_____

3) Is there anyone you've caused harm to that you feel it would be appropriate to confess to them?

_____

_____

_____

4) When you consider the ways you've sinned against these people, how do these thoughts make you feel on a day to day basis?

_____

_____

ashamed, sad, regretful, wish you could undo the damage

5) What response do you hope to get from the individual(s) you plan to confess to?

_____

_____

forgiveness, understanding, a sense of closure

6) How will you handle the situation if you do not get the response you are hoping for? And are you prepared to accept the outcome?

_____

_____

7) What do you hope to gain from confessing to the individuals?

_____

_____

heavy burden lifted, peace, restoration

8) How do you know that confessing to them would be the best thing to do?

_____

_____

CONFESSION AND REPENTANCE

Have you spent time in prayer about this? Have you prayed that God would prepare the individual for hearing your confession?

If you are certain that you must confess this sin to the individual, be confident that you are doing what the Holy Spirit has prompted you to do. Pray, pray, pray, and then pray some more.

JOURNAL

CONFESSION AND REPENTANCE

JOURNAL Week Two Day Six

_____

_____
_____
_____
_____
_____
_____
_____
_____
_____
_____
_____
_____
_____
_____
_____
_____
_____
_____
_____
_____
_____
_____
_____
_____
_____
_____
_____
_____
_____
_____
_____
_____

CONFESSION AND REPENTANCE

TIME FOR ACTION
Week Two Day Seven

☐ I commit to confess my sins to God

☐ I commit to ask God to reveal any unknown sins to me

☐ I commit to pray and ask God to reveal a spiritual mentor/accountability partner to me

☐ I commit to confess and break free from habitual sins

☐ I commit to confess sins perpetrated to others as the Holy Spirit reveals to me

On the next page, jot down any thoughts that you want to share, lessons that you have learned, or revelations of truth about yourself.

JOURNAL

CHAPTER THREE

TO DO

Week Three:

Day One
- ☐ Read the Intro
- ☐ Do the Study Questions
- ☐ Journal

Day Two
- ☐ Read, Ask Forgiveness for Yourself
- ☐ Do the Study Questions
- ☐ Journal

Day Three
- ☐ Read, Forgive Those Who Have Hurt You
- ☐ Do the Study Questions
- ☐ Journal

Day Four
- ☐ Read, Forgive Yourself
- ☐ Do the Study Questions
- ☐ Journal

Day Five
- ☐ Journal

Day Six
- ☐ Journal

Day Seven
- ☐ Time for Action
- ☐ Journal

Chapter 3
FORGIVENESS
Week Three Day One

W hen God began the process of healing in my life, He extended to me the ability to forgive just as He does to us all. However, forgiveness is not an easy choice. When I made the choice to forgive, it came when I realized that I didn't like the bitter, resentful person that I had become. I actually began to despise the person I saw in the mirror.

Unforgiveness was destroying who I was; it was literally killing me from the inside out. Choosing forgiveness, in reality, gave me my life back! I was no longer held captive by bitterness and unforgiveness.

Although I had made the choice to forgive, I began to question whether or not I had truly forgiven. I asked myself, "If I have forgiven why do I still feel the pain from the past?" Whenever I would reflect on my past, I would cry, become depressed, get sad, and feel sorry for the innocent child that I once was, the child who had her safety and security taken from her. I knew that the scriptures said I must forgive in order to be forgiven, so

I really searched my heart to be sure I was being faithful to forgive.

After some time, I began to realize that I had equated the pain, and the memory of what caused the pain, to unforgiveness. I was under the assumption that since I relived all the terrible, painful memories on a daily basis, I must not have truly forgiven the perpetrators of my pain. God revealed to me that forgiveness does not mean that I will forget or stop feeling the pain, and neither does it require that I restore or remain in an unsafe relationship. It just means that I choose to no longer expect punishment for the one who hurt me.

In time, day after day, as I continued to make the choice to forgive, my heart began to heal and the pain eventually became less and less prominent in my daily life.

Because I have learned to forgive, I no longer desire the individuals who've hurt me to be condemned and in actuality I fully hope and pray that they will come to know the Lord and repent for what they have done. Not for me, but for their own salvation.

Forgiveness means I desire salvation rather than retribution.

STUDY

---

1) How has unforgiveness affected your life?

_____

_____

resentfulness, hatefulness, anger, lack of relationship

2) How does unforgiveness affect your self-image?

_____

you may not be the person you really want to be, you may feel disgusted with yourself, you may doubt that you could be loved

3) How can you know that you have forgiven?

_____

_____

when you can love the person who hurt you & desire salvation for them rather than retribution

4) What does it mean to forgive?

_____

_____

to no longer expect punishment

5) How does God help us to forgive?

_____

_____

by reminding us of how we need forgiveness ourselves on a daily basis, and by revealing His grace and mercy to us

6) Does forgiveness require you to restore or remain in an unsafe relationship?

_____

If you are in an abusive situation you must give yourself permission to end the unsafe relationship, get the help you need, and continue to work on forgiveness.

Forgiveness does *NOT* require you to remain in or restore an unsafe relationship.

JOURNAL

_____

_____
_____
_____
_____
_____
_____
_____
_____
_____
_____
_____
_____
_____
_____
_____
_____
_____
_____
_____
_____
_____
_____
_____
_____
_____
_____
_____
_____
_____
_____
_____
_____

ASK FORGIVENESS FOR YOURSELF
Week Three Day Two

As I mentioned in the previous chapter, God will reveal sins to you if you ask Him to. As He reveals those sins to you, you will need to confess and repent as we've already learned, and then ask for forgiveness.

When I confessed to my husband about the things in my past I would not have gotten the closure that I needed if I had not also asked for forgiveness. My husband as well, would not have felt that I was truly sorry for what I had done if I had only confessed these things and not asked him to forgive me. Asking for forgiveness is extremely important. The perfect apology includes confession, repentance, and the request for forgiveness. It is humbling to ask for forgiveness but it is also necessary. You may need to go to an individual or you may just need to go to God, be thorough, search your heart. Go deep while looking for areas in your life that you need forgiveness.

You will learn so much about yourself and who God is, when you reflect on the many ways that you have sinned against Him and then realize that He still forgives you. It can humble you, and help you to appreciate what Christ did on the cross for you. Paul says, in 1Timothy 1:15-16, "Christ Jesus came into the world to save sinners - of whom I am the worst. But for that very reason I was shown mercy so that in me, the worst of sinners,

Christ Jesus might display his unlimited patience as an example for those who would believe on him and receive eternal life."

Your life speaks so much to others and can be your greatest testimony! You may not have persecuted Christians and put them to death as Paul had, but when you face your sins, repent, and ask for forgiveness, it can be life changing for yourself and those around you. As the mercy and grace of God fills your life and begins to transform you, you will naturally begin to share His grace with others.

STUDY

1) Do you have people in your life that you need to ask to forgive you? Who are they and what do you feel you need to ask forgiveness for?

_____

_____

_____

2) What do you need to ask God to forgive you for?

_____

_____

_____

Take the time to reflect on the many ways God has already forgiven you.

3) In what ways does it make it easier for you to forgive others when you see the many ways that you have been forgiven by God?

_____

_____

_____

4) How does it change your attitude on forgiveness toward others? Read Matt. 7:3-5

_____
_____
_____

5) What outward changes happen when you begin to repent and ask for forgiveness?

_____
_____
_____
_____

it's life changing, when the mercy and grace of God fills your life and begins to transform you, you naturally begin to share His mercy and grace with others

JOURNAL

FORGIVE THOSE WHO HURT YOU
Week Three Day Three

You may still hurt, you may still cry, but can you love? Can you find any love at all for the individual who has hurt you?

God is love; He calls us to love others just as He loves us. When you realize that God offers forgiveness to you for even the worst of things that you have done, you should be more willing to forgive those who have sinned against you. After all, none of us are perfect, we're all in need of forgiveness.

"Do not judge, or you too will be judged. For in the same way you judge others, you will be judged, and with the measure you use, it will be measured to you" (Matt. 7:1-2). "Why do you look at the speck of sawdust in your brother's eye and pay no attention to the plank in your own eye? How can you say to your brother, 'Let me take the speck out of your eye,' when all the time there is a plank in your own eye? You hypocrite, first take the plank out of your own eye, and then you will see clearly to remove the speck from your brothers eye" (Matt. 7:3-5). These scriptures do not mean that we become complacent or acceptant of sin, instead they remind us to look at ourselves closely; we are to discover areas in our own lives where we continue to sin.

When we realize that we are sinners as well as those who have hurt us, we should be more willing to forgive. Understand that forgiveness does not mean that you must restore the relatioship and accept a sinful behavior; it just means that you no longer try to punish the individual; you release them and the situation to God and let Him deal with them in His own way. Instead of being resentful and hateful, pray for them so that they may come to a saving relationship with the Lord and finally repent. Jesus died on the cross and let His blood spill to wash away all sin, not just some. Remember that it's sin working in this world and not just a situation, or individual; sin is what has caused your pain.

When I look at my past, I realize that I can hate the sin, but have godly love for the sinner.

I choose to love~
    because when I felt that no one loved me, God did, and it is through that love that I am able to forgive.
I choose to forgive~
    in the hopes that by forgiving, I can reveal God's love to the one who has hurt me.
I forgive for God~
    because He is faithful to forgive me.
I forgive for myself~
    because, when I was full of unforgiveness, I was hateful and I desired to love again.

Truly, you forgive for yourself, not for the individual. But out of that forgiveness grows a desire to see the salvation of the person whom you have forgiven. When you forgive for yourself you realize that you are able to forgive even the unrepentant person. The following story is an example of this:

In October, 2006, my mother revealed to me that the stepbrother who had abused me was suffering from a terminal disease and was near death. While I was on the phone with my mom, I began to cry, silent tears, (because, I didn't want to upset my mom). I was crying for several reasons.

First, I had forgiven my stepbrother but I had always hoped that someday I would be able to look him in the eyes and possibly see repentance. I had not seen or spoken to him since I was eleven, during the time when he had abused me. In fact, he had moved away without ever saying good-bye. In that moment, as my mother revealed his fate, I realized that I will never know if he is sorry for what he did or even if he is aware of how it affected my life.

Second, my heart was saddened by the awareness that I have no idea whether he will see heaven when he dies. Had he accepted Christ as his Savior? Had he repented and asked forgiveness for his sins? Did he ever know the love of the Lord? During his final month, I had to find comfort in the knowledge that I won't have the answer to those questions until I am in Heaven.

I had to be secure in forgiveness as something I did for myself, not because my stepbrother asked for or even deserved it (as none of us actually deserve forgiveness), but because God has required it of me. Also, I needed to know that I didn't have to tell him that I forgave him; in fact doing so may have caused more harm than good. Especially, if he was unaware of what sin he had committed. If he had asked for forgiveness, then it would make sense to tell him that yes, indeed, I have forgiven him. However, in this situation, all that I could do was pray for him.

He died on Thanksgiving Day, 2006, and I truly hope to see him in heaven some day.

You may also have to forgive an unrepentant person. Therefore, you need to be secure knowing that you are forgiving for yourself not for them. You are forgiving so that "you will be forgiven" (Luke 6:37). Let God take care of those who've hurt you. He desires for them to come to know Him just as He desired the same for you, so pray for them. "Pray for those who mistreat you" (Luke 6:28). You may never get the chance to see the person come to know the Lord and they may never repent and ask you to forgive them. They may not even be aware that they need you to forgive them. All you can do is freely offer forgiveness and pray for their salvation in the Lord. The rest is in Gods hands, find peace with that.

A wonderful story of forgiveness is found in the testimony of Corrie Ten Boom. As a former prisoner of a German concentration camp, she lost both her father and sister during the ten months that they were all imprisoned. After being released from Ravensbruck, she began to speak all over Germany to share the message of forgiveness. While speaking at one of these events, she came face to face with one of the guards of Ravensbruck.

In a Guidepost article from 1972, titled I'm Still Learning to Forgive[1], Corrie shares her story of being confronted head on with the challenge to forgive even when she didn't feel like it. The following is an excerpt from that article:

"It was in a church in Munich that I saw him, a balding heavy-set man in a grey overcoat, a brown felt hat clutched between his hands. People were filing out of the basement room where I had just spoken. It was 1947 and I had come from Holland to defeated Germany with the message that God forgives. ...

"And that's when I saw him, working his way forward against the others. One moment I saw the overcoat and the brown hat; the next, a blue uniform and a visored cap with its skull and crossbones. It came back with a rush: the huge room with its harsh overhead lights, the pathetic pile of dresses and shoes in the center of the floor, the shame of walking naked past this

FORGIVENESS

man. I could see my sister's frail form ahead of me, ribs sharp beneath the parchment skin. Betsie, how thin you were!

"Betsie and I had been arrested for concealing Jews in our home during the Nazi occupation of Holland; this man had been a guard at Ravensbruck concentration camp where we were sent. …

"'You mentioned Ravensbruck in your talk,' he was saying. 'I was a guard in there.' No, he did not remember me. 'But since that time,' he went on, 'I have become a Christian. I know that God has forgiven me for the cruel things I did there, but I would like to hear it from your lips as well. Fraulein, …' his hand came out, … 'will you forgive me?'

"And I stood there, I whose sins had every day to be forgiven, and could not. Betsie had died in that place, could he erase her slow terrible death simply for the asking?

"It could not have been many seconds that he stood there, hand held out, but to me it seemed hours as I wrestled with the most difficult thing I had ever had to do.

"For I had to do it, I knew that. The message that God forgives has a prior condition: that we forgive those who have injured us. 'If you do not forgive men their trespasses,' Jesus says, 'neither will your Father in heaven forgive your trespasses.'

…

FORGIVENESS

"And still I stood there with the coldness clutching my heart. But forgiveness is not an emotion, I knew that too. Forgiveness is an act of the will, and the will can function regardless of the temperature of the heart. 'Jesus, help me!' I prayed silently. 'I can lift my hand, I can do that much. You supply the feeling.'

"And so woodenly, mechanically, I thrust my hand into the one stretched out to me. And as I did, an incredible thing took place. The current started in my shoulder, raced down my arm, sprang into our joined hands. And then this healing warmth seemed to flood my whole being, bringing tears to my eyes.

"'I forgive you, brother!' I cried. 'With all my heart!'"

When I read her story, I can just feel the healing that transpired on that day, for both of them. In the same article, Corrie shared that she had never known God's love so intensely as she did the moment she held hands with the guard and forgave him. What an amazing testimony of forgiveness and healing, and what a blessing to be given the opportunity to walk through that forgiveness face to face with the one who had hurt her.

An important thing to notice is that it was only after she made the choice to forgive and actually placed her hand in his, that the feeling of forgiveness and healing came.

A repentant heart does make forgiveness easier, but regardless of whether or not the individual ever asks for forgiveness, you must forgive in order to find healing. Remember, forgiveness is a choice. You may not have the feelings yet, but in time, when you make the daily choice to forgive, the healing of forgiveness will come.

STUDY

---

1) What does it mean to love?

_____

Read Matt. 7:12 and Matt. 5:43-48

2) What does it mean to love others as yourself?

_____

_____

3) How can you love the one who has hurt you?

_____

_____

Review the following section from the book.

*I choose to **love**~*
> because when I felt that no one loved me, God did, and it is through that love that I am able to forgive.

I choose to forgive~
> in the hopes that by forgiving, I can reveal Gods love to the one who has hurt me.

I forgive for God~
> because He is faithful to forgive me.

I forgive for myself~

because, when I was full of unforgiveness, I was hateful and I desired to **love** again.

4) What does this paragraph say to you?

_____

love and forgiveness are choices, they go hand in hand

FORGIVENESS

5) Why should you choose to love? Read Matt. 22:36-40

_____

Read Matt. 22:36-40, it's the greatest commandment.

6) Why should you choose to forgive? Read Mark 11:25

_____

_____

Read Mark 11:25, you forgive so that your sins will be forgiven

7) Why do you forgive for God?

_____

because He commands us to, because He offers forgiveness to us

8) Why do you forgive for yourself?

_____

so that you can be forgiven, so that you can reveal God's love and grace to the one whom you have forgiven, so that you won't be taken over by resentfulness
Love and forgiveness are both choices; when you make the decision to do one, it makes the other one easier.
Do you see the cycle and how it all begins and ends with love?
Love and forgiveness go hand in hand.

9) How do you feel about forgiving an unrepentant person?

_____

_____

10) How did you feel after reading about the unrepentant step brother?

_____

_____

_____

11) Do you think it is necessary to tell an unrepentant person that you forgive them? Why or why not?

_____

_____

_____

12) What must you do in order to forgive an unrepentant person?

_____

_____

Choose to forgive, recognize that forgiveness is something you do because God has required it, not because the person deserves it or even asked for it? Remember that none of us "deserve" forgiveness but God still offers it. The grace and mercy that God has shown us, requires that we extend grace and mercy to others.

13) How did you feel after reading the testimony of Corrie Ten Boom, the prisoner of a concentration camp?

_____

_____

_____

14) In what ways did the guard's actions make her forgiveness easier?

_____

he was repentant, humble, and he asked her for forgiveness

15) In what ways did it make her forgiveness harder?

_____

she had to face the memories and pain, and make the decision right then and there to forgive him face to face regardless of what she was feeling at that moment

16) Was it still her choice to forgive?

_____

17) What could have happened if she had refused to offer
    forgiveness?

_____

_____

_____

_____

18) When did she actually "feel" the healing that took place?

_____

_____

after she made the decision to forgive and placed her hand in his
We must make the decision to forgive first and then the
feelings of forgiveness will follow. It is a daily choice to
forgive.

JOURNAL

_____
_____
_____
_____
_____
_____
_____
_____
_____
_____
_____
_____
_____
_____
_____
_____
_____
_____
_____
_____
_____
_____
_____
_____
_____
_____
_____
_____
_____
_____
_____
_____
_____
_____

FORGIVENESS

FORGIVE YOURSELF
Week Three Day Four

The final thing you need to do when you are dealing with forgiveness, is forgive yourself. This is sometimes the hardest thing to do. It can be easier to ask for forgiveness than it is to accept it, but part of forgiving yourself is accepting the forgiveness that Christ Jesus offers you.

In my case, I forgave myself for not guarding my purity and for not placing a high value on my life. I forgave myself for being self abusive through the use of drugs and alcohol. Ultimately, I forgave myself for sinning against the Lord.

Don't consider forgiving yourself to be of less importance. In fact, it may be the greatest stumbling block for you if you are unable to accomplish this task. When you deny yourself forgiveness, it's just as detrimental as holding a grudge against someone else. The same blood that was shed for the ones that hurt you also covers your own sins, and when you are unable to forgive yourself, it's as if you are saying that Christ's blood on the cross was not enough to free you from your sins. C.S. Lewis said, "I think if God forgives us we must forgive ourselves otherwise it is almost like setting up ourselves as a higher tribunal than Him."[2]

God has the ultimate authority to judge and punish you and yet He forgives you once you accept His Son as your Savior.

Why then, are you still punishing yourself and deciding that you are undeserving of forgiveness? What causes you to resent, despise, or hate yourself so much that you feel you shouldn't be forgiven? Is it impossible for you to imagine yourself as already forgiven by the one who matters most?

If you know that God has forgiven you, are you considering yourself to be greater than God when you deny forgiveness for yourself? I believe so. Forgiving yourself does not need to be a stumbling block for you. If you can learn to accept God's forgiveness you can learn to forgive yourself. If you are unable to complete this step, you will continue to beat yourself up inside and Satan will maintain his foothold. Claiming forgiveness for yourself will lead to deeper and more complete healing, and is vital to continued freedom.

As you can see, forgiveness involves many things, each one is of equal importance. Make all aspects of forgiveness a priority in your life, and ultimately, be willing to forgive yourself.

STUDY

1) Why is forgiving yourself so hard?

_____

_____

2) Why is it important to forgive yourself?

_____

because God commands us to forgive, and that includes our self

3) What effect does your inability to forgive yourself have on your life?

_____

_____

Remember it's the same blood that was shed for all sin, including your own. If you are unable to forgive yourself, it's as if you are   saying that Christ's blood was not enough to cover your sins.

When God commands you to forgive others so that you may be forgiven, He also wants you to forgive yourself. Forgiveness is extremely important in order for healing to take place.

4) What obstacles are keeping you from fully offering or accepting your own forgiveness?

_____

_____

5) Do you think you deserve to be forgiven? Why or Why not?

_____

_____

6) Which do you find is easier to do, forgiving others or forgiving yourself?

_____

7) In regards to the last question, what makes the one easier than the other?

_____

_____

_____

_____

JOURNAL

JOURNAL Week Three Day Five

_____

_____
_____
_____
_____
_____
_____
_____
_____
_____
_____
_____
_____
_____
_____
_____
_____
_____
_____
_____
_____
_____
_____
_____
_____
_____
_____
_____
_____
_____
_____

FORGIVENESS

JOURNAL Week Three Day Six

_____

_____
_____
_____
_____
_____
_____
_____
_____
_____
_____
_____
_____
_____
_____
_____
_____
_____
_____
_____
_____
_____
_____
_____
_____
_____
_____
_____
_____
_____
_____
_____
_____
_____
_____

FORGIVENESS

TIME FOR ACTION
Week Three Day Seven

- ☐ I commit to ask God for forgiveness
- ☐ I commit to ask others to forgive me
- ☐ I commit to forgive those who've sinned against me
- ☐ I commit to accept God's forgiveness
- ☐ I commit to forgive myself

On the next page, jot down any thoughts that you want to share, lessons that you have learned, or revelations of truth about yourself.

JOURNAL

_____
_____
_____
_____
_____
_____
_____
_____
_____
_____
_____
_____
_____
_____
_____
_____
_____
_____
_____
_____
_____
_____
_____
_____
_____
_____
_____
_____
_____
_____
_____
_____
_____

CHAPTER FOUR

TO DO

Week Four:

Day One
- ☐ Read the Intro
- ☐ Do the Study Questions
- ☐ Journal

Day Two
- ☐ Read, Heavenly Father vs. Earthly Father
- ☐ Do the Study Questions
- ☐ Journal

Day Three
- ☐ Read, When People Let You Down
- ☐ Do the Study Questions
- ☐ Journal

Day Four
- ☐ Read, Dealing with Abandonment
- ☐ Do the Study Questions
- ☐ Journal

Day Five
- ☐ Read, Give God Control
- ☐ Do the Study Questions
- ☐ Journal

Day Six
- ☐ Journal

Day Seven
- ☐ Time for Action
- ☐ Journal

Chapter 4
TRUST AND CONTROL
Week Four Day One

Whan I was a child I dreamt of having a father that would dance with me. I wanted a father I could hug and feel safe within his arms, one that could have lifted me up on his lap and I wouldn't have been frightened. I simply desired a father that would protect me from harm. In reality, however, I never had that kind of relationship with either of my fathers.

My biological father was a hateful, abusive, and selfish man. A Narcissist, he was either the hero or the victim (at least in his own eyes and how he portrayed himself), there was no healthy in-between. He wanted the world to see him as some kind of hero but wasn't one to his own family. He lied continuously to anyone he came in contact with, and because of that I can honestly say that I, myself, really never knew him.

My parents got divorced before my birth, and it was a painful divorce because of the hatred between the two of them. My father had abused my mother in so many horrible ways, I cannot even begin to mention them. The hatred my mother had for him was the result of that abuse. He was also verbally and physically abusive to my sisters and I when we would visit him on the weekends. I remember when I was four and I was dropped off at my grandmother's house after spending the weekend with my dad. My grandmother was shocked by my face. I had red handprints on both of my cheeks from where my father had come from behind and smacked both of my ears. To add insult to injury, I had a lot trouble with my ears as a child and was pretty much deaf until I had my first set of tubes put in at the age of four. My dad would also ridicule and humiliate me in front of other people. This set me up for a lifetime of self doubt, and insecurity, making me vulnerable to future abuses.

When I was about seven years old we stopped visiting my dad on the weekends and we moved out of town. From that moment on, we never heard from him again (until we contacted him as adults). No birthday cards, phone calls or anything. It was as if he had dropped off the face of the earth.

Over the years, however, I began to put my dad on a pedestal, especially when life began to get tough for me. As a way to escape reality, I would imagine him as this wonderful, perfect dad who missed us terribly and just couldn't find us for some unknown reason. Somehow, I had forgotten how abusive he was. I just knew there must be some good explanation for why he had abandoned us. Unfortunately, these thoughts were far from accurate.

The truth was, my father's pride kept him from us. He bragged later in life, as I began to try to build a relationship with him, that he always knew where we were and what we were up to. That was the "hero" side of him. On the other hand, when the situation called for it, I would see the "victim" side of him. For example, when I talked about how he never called or sent birthday cards to my sisters and I, he would say that he had no

TRUST AND CONTROL

idea where we were, no way to contact us, and talk about how he missed out on so much of our lives. I began to learn that the situation determined his excuse. What ever put him in the best light, that is what I would hear.

The lack of relationship with my biological father caused me to draw closer to my stepdad when I was very young and he became my replacement father. I followed him everywhere, until the day he began to abuse me. At that moment, all of my dreams of a happy, healthy, father-daughter relationship died.

Although in time I was able to forgive my biological father and my step father, I still had been let down by both of them and that affected my ability to trust. So then, as I began to build a relationship with my Heavenly Father, as you can imagine, it was very difficult to get past my lack of trust. I was afraid that if I allowed God into the deepest part of my heart, the only outcome would be more pain because I was certain He would let me down too.

So with all this in mind, let me ask you some questions. How do you define a father? What qualities do you think of when you think of a father? How do you know what makes a good father when all the information you have gathered on the subject has come from an unhealthy source? Or what if you've never had a father figure in your life? I know a lot of questions, but let me share with you some words that I think could define or describe a father.

A Father is a Provider *(Gen. 22:14)*, Protector *(Ps. 41:2)*, Healer *(Ex. 15:26)*, Comforter *(Isa. 51:12)*, and Teacher *(Job 36:22)*. He is Safety *(Ps. 4:8)* and Strength *(Ps. 18:1)*. A Father teaches us about love *(Lam. 3:22)*, affection *(Phil. 1:8)*, honesty, truth *(Isa. 65:16)*, trust *(Dan. 6:23; Prov. 3:5)*, compassion *(Isa. 54:10)*, hope *(Jer. 29:11)*, and obedience *(Heb. 5:8-9)*. A Father loves us unconditionally, and forgives us even when we don't feel that we deserve it *(Ps. 103:3)*. He would do anything in his power to take away our pain or suffering *(Rev. 21:4)*. He would be willing to set aside his own needs in order to supply ours *(Matt. 26:39; John 3:16)*. He has plans for our future, and sees the best in us even when we don't see good in ourselves *(Ex. 3:11; Jer. 1:6-7)*.

There is only one Father who perfectly and completely matches the description I've given you and that is God the Father. He wants you to know that He is your perfect Father and you can trust Him!

STUDY

1) When you think of the word father what descriptive words come to mind?

_____

_____

2) What kind of relationship do you have with your father or father figure?

_____

share your own personal story

3) In what ways is it a healthy or unhealthy relationship?

_____

4) What are the qualities of a good father?

_____

_____

_____

5) How has your relationship with your father shaped your relationships with other people or with members of the opposite sex?

_____

_____

_____

_____

6) How has it affected your relationship with your Heavenly
Father?

_____

_____

7) Take time to read the verses listed below. What do these
verses tell you about the attributes of God?
see the last paragraph before the study questions for the answers

Gen. 22:14 _____

Ps. 41:2 _____

Ex. 15:26 _____

Isa. 51:12 _____

Job 36:22 _____

Ps. 4:8 _____

Ps. 18:1 _____

Lam. 3:22 _____

Phil. 1:8 _____

Isa. 65:16 _____

Dan. 6:23; Prov. 3:5 _____

Isa. 54:10 _____

Jer. 29:11 _____

Heb. 5:8-9 _____

Ps. 103:3 _____

Rev. 21:4 _____

Matt. 26:39; John 3:16 _____

Ex. 3:11; Jer. 1:6-7 _____

JOURNAL

HEAVENLY FATHER VS. EARTHLY FATHER
Week Four Day Two

On day one of this chapter, I attempted to come up with as many descriptions of the "ideal" father that I could. I hope that you took the time to read the scripture verses that were referenced with each word. This is just a sampling of the scriptures that refer to the character of God! So the question that I ask is this, could this be coincidence? I don't think so. I think that it's a perfectly accurate description of who God is. He is our Heavenly Father. That is not just a catch phrase, it is the truth! He is our Creator and we are His children. He is our Abba, Father! "For you did not receive a spirit that makes you a slave again to fear, but you received the Spirit of sonship. And by him we cry, 'Abba, Father.' The Spirit himself testifies with our spirit that we are God's children. Now if we are children, then we are heirs, heirs of God and co-heirs with Christ, if indeed we share in his sufferings in order that we may also share in his glory" (Rom. 8:15-17).

If you look up the definition for the word Abba, you will find that the word is translated into the English language as "father, my father, or our father." The word was used in biblical times by Jesus and early Christians to address God. You will discover in your search that the word suggests familial intimacy, and isn't that exactly what God wants us to have with Him, intimacy? He desires to spend time with us and He gives us His full attention. He is 'El Roi', which means, the God who sees me. He gives us the desires of our hearts. It is because of His unending love for us, that we are able to truly love others. He is our example, our knight in shining armor who comes to rescue us.

What a wonderful Father that we have in Him. Your earthly father may have let you down, but God, your Heavenly Father, will never let you down. He will never hurt you and He will never abandon you. "No one will be able to stand up against you all the days of your life. As I was with Moses, so I will be with you; I will never leave you nor forsake you" (Josh. 1:5). "Though my father and mother forsake me, the Lord will receive me" (Ps. 27:10). You can trust Him and let Him begin to heal you from deep within the most hidden parts of your heart! You can feel whole because you are part of a loving family and you have a father who truly and perfectly loves you unconditionally. And most importantly, you can feel wanted and cared for by a father who adores you and has plans for you that are far beyond what you could ever hope for or imagine!

STUDY

1) Do you think it is possible for anyone other than God to be the "ideal" father as described earlier? _____

2) What does that tell you about God?

_____

He truly is our perfect Heavenly Father!

3) How does it change the way you look at God when you realize that He truly is your Heavenly Father?

_____

TRUST AND CONTROL

4) God is our "Abba Father." Based on the definition of Abba, what does that statement tell you about our relationship with God?

We're His children, heirs of God and co-heirs with Christ. He desires to have familial intimacy with us. He wants to spend time with us.

5) Is it difficult for you to think of God as your Heavenly Father? What makes it difficult?

_____

_____

_____

6) We've learned that God will never let you down or hurt you, so are you able to trust Him? Why or Why not? Read Deut. 31:6; Josh. 1:5

_____

_____

7) How does it feel to know that you have a Father in Heaven who truly loves you and wants the best for you regardless of anything you've done in the past? He loves you unconditionally.

_____

_____

_____

_____

_____

JOURNAL

WHEN PEOPLE LET YOU DOWN
Week Four Day Three

A few years ago, I was at a retreat and the speaker asked us all to close our eyes. He instructed us to think about what God looks like. He wanted us to see the picture that would formulate in our mind of what God looked like to us personally. When I did this, I saw Jesus reaching His hand down to pull me out of a well. The well was lined in brick and it seemed too tall for me to climb over by myself, so I was just stuck in the lonely, cold, darkness of this well. Above me I saw a bright light streaming in, with Jesus on His knees reaching His hand down into the well. He was stretching as far as He could to reach me, but He needed me to reach up to Him so that He could lift me out. The interesting thing about this picture was that at this point in time, I was just beginning to recognize that I had built up a "wall of protection" that was preventing God from truly entering the deepest part of my heart. Sadly, I had not yet discovered how to break it down.

I had been hurt so many times by people in the past that I began to treat God like I did all of my relationships. If I felt that someone was getting too close to me, I would pull back and retreat into my wall of protection. When I would make a new friend, I would really spend a lot of quality time with them in order to establish the relationship, and then I would start to panic inside, afraid that I would get hurt. That same panic would cause me to suddenly cut back on phone calls and I would stop spending as much time with them. They would begin wondering if I was mad at them, or if they had done something wrong. Of course, they hadn't done anything, I was just scared. I think the panic came from the fear of people seeing me for what I felt that I truly was, "damaged goods." I felt that my life was so screwed up and if people were to really get to know me, they would see all the bad in me and then reject me. At the same time, I had myself convinced that if I kept God at a distance He wouldn't be able to see all the deep, hidden things in my heart. I would go back and forth from wanting a close relationship with Him to pushing Him away and avoiding Him. I didn't want God to get too close either. In other words, I pushed everyone away.

The wall of protection I had built for myself was actually alienating me from everyone, including the one who would truly never hurt me. God was on the outside of that wall just waiting for me to reach up to Him so that He could pull me out. While I was "safe and protected" within the walls of my personal well, I was actually very cold and lonely, and I had separated myself from the warmth of the light of God's presence. Of course, I was not aware of what the so called "walls of protection" were actually robbing me of. In my mind, I was safe from being hurt.

The irony is, because of the narrowness of my well, or "wall," I allowed unsafe people to get too close to me, and I still got hurt. The very thing that was supposed to protect me didn't even prevent that from happening. It did however; keep me from developing healthy, strong relationships.

I needed to learn how to set up healthy boundaries; boundaries that allow safe people to come inside while still allowing me the distance to recognize an unsafe person or situation before they have the ability to hurt me so deeply. I also had to learn to trust people, and most importantly, God.

TRUST AND CONTROL

When you begin to build a relationship with someone you start out with faith, faith that they will be a trustworthy person. You give them the chance to "earn" your trust. "Whoever can be trusted with very little can also be trusted with much, and whoever is dishonest with very little will also be dishonest with much" (Luke 16:10). If a person shows you that they can be trusted with little then let them be trusted with much. Let time in the relationship reveal their character. Does the individual judge others, gossip, or share other people's secrets? Or do they show that they have integrity and can be trusted? Do they reveal God's love to others by treating people the way they themselves would want to be treated? Have faith in someone first and let them earn your trust. Faith says that you believe in them before seeing their trustworthiness, while trust is something that is proven and earned. Trust also has the ability to be lost, gained, and regained. Learn to adjust your boundary according to how much trust the individual has earned from you.

You must realize that people will let you down. Of course we are all guilty of that at times. Regardless of this fact, try to let safe, trustworthy people into your life enough that when they do let you down, there is enough room to forgive them and repair the relationship. Shallow relationships are hard to restore, there is no substance to them, and they have no intrinsic value to us so it is easy for us to give up on them. Alternatively, relationships that you value are worth the work that it takes to restore them and rebuild trust.

Shortly after God began to work on me in this area of trust, I was tested in it. I had a friendship that I had allowed myself to be vulnerable in. It was the first time in a long time that I had actually been able to be this close to a person because I had been hurt in previous relationships. I was treading on shaky ground because of my own fears of being hurt, but I still allowed myself to trust this friend.

TRUST AND CONTROL

Then, we had a disagreement and a lot of hurtful words of judgment were spoken by her. This of course, hit right at the core of my insecurity. As I shared earlier, I felt that if people got too close to me they would see my imperfections and then reject me because of them. So here I was, face to face with the very thing that had previously kept me far from God and my relationships with others; the lack of ability to trust.

My first instinct was to build that wall up again. However, I recognized this in myself immediately so I did try, within the first week or so, to reach out to her and try to restore the relationship. Unfortunately, the injury was too tender for both of us at that moment so I had to step away from the relationship for a time and process what had happened.

I realized that we are all imperfect and just as I didn't want to be judged for my imperfections I also could not judge my friend for hers. "You, therefore, have no excuse, you who pass judgment on someone else, for at whatever point you judge another, you are condemning yourself, because you who pass judgment do the same things" (Rom. 2:1). We are all imperfect after all. I knew that I valued our friendship, but I also needed to take some time away from the relationship to allow myself to heal from the hurtful words. I had to forgive her and let God use this time to teach me something about myself.

Whenever I am dealing with a difficult situation, I always try to ask God, "What do you want me to learn from this?" What I learned through this situation is that you need to set different boundaries with different people. Boundaries are based on trust and safety in the relationship and can change as the relationship grows and as you get to know each other better. The more time you spend in a relationship you should begin to learn about the individual, and how trustworthy they are. Let their character and integrity determine how close you let them into your boundary. You don't have to trust everyone, but you should still be able to trust. Don't let past hurts keep you from being able to trust anyone at all.

If you were to ask me, I would say that taking a risk of getting hurt in a healthy relationship is far better than having a false sense of safety behind a wall and being all alone and trapped within it. The key is to recognize the unhealthy relationships and cherish the healthy ones. Set up healthy boundaries and learn to recognize those people that you can trust and allow into your boundary, and keep those you can't trust at a distance.

Another thing that I have learned in allowing myself to trust, is that I never knew how loved I could feel until I allowed God to fully enter my life. Trust God, He will never hurt you or let you down. I am fully aware of His love for me each and every day, and my heart is warmed by His presence within me. Even when I accepted the Lord as my Savior, I had still never truly felt the completeness of His love for me until I learned to trust Him. I am so thankful that He loved me enough to reach down to pull me out of the well and that I finally learned to trust Him enough to reach up. What is keeping you from reaching up to Him?

STUDY

Close your eyes and think about what God looks like to you.
1) Describe what you see.

_____

_____

_____

2) What does that image say to you? What personal meaning can you find in that image?

_____

_____

_____

TRUST AND CONTROL

3) In what ways can you relate to the image that I saw and shared in the story?

_____

_____

_____

4) In what ways are you pushing God away?

_____

_____

_____

5) In what ways are you pushing people away?

_____

_____

_____

6) What things can you do in order to develop healthy strong relationships?

_____

learn to trust, realize that you alone can determine how you set your boundaries with each individual, remember not everyone will hurt you

7) Why is it difficult for you to trust?

_____

_____

_____

8) How can you begin to trust people? Read Luke 16:10-12

_____

The more time you spend in a relationship you should begin to learn about the individual, and how trustworthy they are. Let

their character and integrity determine how close you let them into your boundary. You don't have to trust everyone, but you should still be able to trust. Don't let past hurts keep you from being able to trust anyone at all.

9) What can you do in order to begin trusting God?

_____

Believe what the bible teaches you about who God is, remember all that you have read about Him. Review the scriptures that were referenced in this book. Spend time with Him and get to know Him.

10) What do you usually do when you trust someone and they let you down?

_____

_____

11) What should you do if you decide that you need (or want) to maintain the relationship with someone who has broken your trust?

_____

_____

_____

Regardless of whether you wish to restore the relationship, you must realize that we are all imperfect and offer grace and forgiveness to the individual. Recognize it will take time to heal the hurts; adjust your boundaries until they earn your trust again.

12) Have you ever had a relationship in which you were able to be completely vulnerable? Explain.

_____

_____

_____

13) What has happened to that relationship? Is it still a healthy one?

_____

_____

_____

14) If it's still healthy, what has kept it that way?

_____

_____

_____

15) If your relationship was lost, what have you learned from the experience?

_____

_____

_____

16) Do you agree with the following statement? "Taking a risk of getting hurt in a healthy relationship is far better than having a false sense of safety behind a wall and being all alone and trapped within it." Why or why not?

_____

_____

Remind them to recognize unhealthy relationships and cherish the healthy ones, set up healthy boundaries.

17) Are you ready to trust God and reach up to Him so that He can pull you out of that well? If not, what is keeping you from it?

_____

_____

_____

JOURNAL

DEALING WITH ABANDONMENT
Week Four Day Four

When dealing with trust issues, something else that can prevent you from trusting God is the feeling of abandonment. When my real father had not communicated with my sisters and I as children and never tried to see us, I had to deal with abandonment. And again, when I was 16, the year that I was kicked out of my parent's house, I spent Thanksgiving, Christmas, Easter, and my 17th birthday alone. I didn't see or hear from my mom for several months and even beyond that I had not been allowed to participate in any family celebrations for over a year. I really felt abandoned.

When I think of abandonment, I am also reminded of a situation that I observed about 13 years ago. I was on my way to work early in the morning, and far ahead of me there was a car that had pulled over to the side of the road. It was still somewhat dark and I was several yards away from them when suddenly they peeled away from the side of the road and sped down the highway.

As I got closer to the spot where they had been, I could see the dog that they had just dumped, running in desperation to catch up with them. Then, suddenly, the dog stopped, turned around to look behind him and then looked back toward the car that had just left. He once again tried to chase after them for a bit and finally he just gave up and watched them leave.

I pulled up along side of the dog and tried to coax him into my car. I could see the confusion on his face and his look of desperation. Unfortunately, I could not gain his trust and he disappeared into the cornfield.

My heart ached for that dog, who at one time must have been wanted and loved by his family, but for some unknown reason was now being tossed aside and abandoned. He probably made some mistakes, got into some trouble and his owners didn't know how to deal with him. What really impacted me was the fact that as I offered him help, he refused it. Here comes the word "trust" again! This dog's trust had been compromised and he was so confused by the abandonment, that he could not recognize the help being presented to him.

If you have had to deal with feelings of abandonment, you probably also tend to refuse help. You probably have this sense of, "I don't need anyone, I can make it on my own." You are afraid to rely on anyone else because they may leave you and then you'll be left to go it alone again. You have gotten used to carrying the entire burden by yourself. Honestly in your opinion, it's easier to maintain the momentum of carrying it all by yourself because eventually you'd have to pick it up again when they let you down.

I understand that feeling, because I used to feel the same way. One of the big problems with that way of thinking is that you can get worn out and exhausted from going it alone. You need to recognize that there are people who can help you carry the burden and that God will never abandon you, He will never forsake you, He will never let you down.

God can put people in your path that you can and should rely on, ask Him to help you to recognize those people. Also, as the following verses reveal, God will never abandon you. "Be strong and courageous. Do not be afraid or terrified because of them, for the Lord your God goes with you; He will never leave you nor forsake you" (Deut. 31:6). "The Lord himself goes before you and will be with you, he will never leave you nor forsake you[...]" (Deut. 31:8), and "[...]because God has said, 'Never will I leave you; never will I forsake you'" (Heb. 13:5). Once you realize that God will not abandon you, it will be easier for you to release your burdens ultimately to Him and then move on to the next step, which is giving God control.

STUDY

1) Have you ever felt abandoned? Describe the situation.

_____

_____

_____

2) In what ways can you relate to the story of the abandoned dog?

_____

_____

_____

3) Have your feelings of abandonment caused you to refuse help from outsiders? _____

4) In what ways have you been offered help and how did you refuse it?

_____

_____

_____

_____

_____

TRUST AND CONTROL

5) Do you see how God has placed people in your path that have offered to help carry some of your burdens? Who are they?

_____

_____

_____

6) Can you see, after reading the following verses Ps. 94:14; Deut. 31:6 & 8; 1 Chron. 28:20; and Hebrews 13:5, that God will never abandon you? How does that make you feel?

_____

_____

_____

7) Do you think you will be able to release your burdens to Him once and for all? Why or why not?

_____

_____

_____

JOURNAL

GIVE GOD CONTROL
Week Four Day Five

Give God control of my life! What does that mean? So am I
supposed to be a puppet under God's control?

Are these the questions you are asking when you think of
giving God control? I know it is hard to imagine giving up
something that has been so important to you.

When life throws things out of control, you may try to
maintain a sense of sanity by controlling things around you.
Some things that you may be trying to control are the way you
organize your house, schedule, and the way you control your
relationships. Just like I used to control how close I would allow
people to get to me, you are probably controlling your friends,
family and opposite sex relationships. When life seems chaotic,
do you get overly focused on those things that you think you
have the ability to control? Are you being affected by an
obsessive compulsive behavior? Do you get freaked out by things
that are going the wrong way? Do you even control your
emotions so that people won't see the reality of your lack of
control? Do you attempt to direct life instead of letting life just
happen and trusting that God is in control? A ton of questions I
know, but there are many ways the feeling of a lack of control
can affect you.

It just about drives me crazy to watch old family videos

because I remember feeling so uptight about everything being just perfect. I never wanted to fail or to appear unable to handle the stress of the birthday party, or Christmas dinner, or any other family event. I recall a video of my sons 6th birthday party, he was having so much fun opening his presents and his friends were excited to see him open that special gift that they had selected just for him. Today when I watch that video I am ashamed of the way I sound. I was criticizing my husband for not helping with all the discarded wrapping paper and I was commanding my son not to open the box to begin playing with the toy that he just opened because he might lose the parts. Instead of just enjoying the time with my family and watching my sons excitement as he was receiving these wonderful new things, I was worried about losing control of the situation. My life had been so full of things that were out of my control, that I had taken on the habit of trying to control the people and situations around me, I became an annoying perfectionist.

There is a problem with being a perfectionist. The reality is, no one is ever perfect, nor can you expect life to be. Even though you want perfection, you are fighting a losing battle. Of course, there are some things in life where a person might need to strive for perfection, such as driving a car, performing surgery, or flying a plane, but all they can really do is try their best. So no matter how much you may try, ultimately, you are unable to keep everything perfect because there are too many variables that are out of your control. For instance, while driving you cannot predict whether the person in the semi, coming at you from the opposite direction, has had enough rest and is alert enough to control his vehicle and stay in his lane. You cannot control what he is doing. What you can do is make sure that you are prepared to drive safely and maintain the correct speed, etc. Just as equally, you may have had all the routine maintenance done on your vehicle but still blow a tire and lose control, hitting the oncoming semi. The point is, life happens and certain things are out of your control, whether bad or good, regardless of your efforts to maintain complete control and keep things perfect in your life.

Giving God control of your life will not cause everything to spin out of control, it will not cause everything to fall apart. Regardless of what you may have believed in the past, you will not lose control by giving God control. Neither, will giving God control mean that bad things will never happen to you again, that is not reality. You have no control over what other people say, do, or think. You can only control those things that you say, do, or think. So when someone hurts you, realize that you could not do anything to prevent it, but you can choose to give that situation to God and let Him be in control of it.

This is where trust becomes very important. Romans 8:28 says, "In all things, God works for the good of those who love him." Trust God and give Him complete control of your life. Even when bad things are happening, you need to remember that verse, memorize it and repeat it to yourself when you are struggling to give God control of every situation. All you need to do is simply say, "God, I give you control of my life and my circumstances," and mean it from the bottom of your heart. Be honest and tell Him if you don't know exactly how to give Him control, He will help you. Don't worry, there are no "puppet" strings attached!

Simply put, giving God control means that you are recognizing that you cannot be perfect, your life is not going to be perfect, and you trust that God is in control, has your best interest at heart, and has a purpose for everything. When you are burdened, tell God about it, and release it to Him, trust that He is taking care of it.

Rely on God, trust in Him, believe that He will never abandon you, and give Him complete control.

TRUST AND CONTROL

STUDY

---

1) Are you afraid of giving God control? Why?

_____

_____

afraid of what it means, fear of losing free will, fear of losing control

2) What does control mean to you?

_____

safety, security etc.

3) What things in your life do you try to maintain control of?

_____

_____

relationships, people, situations, cleanliness, are you OCD, etc.

4) What do you think will happen if you stop trying to control all of these things?

_____

_____

5) Is it realistic to think that you can truly maintain control of those things? Why or why not?

_____

_____

6) How does your attempt to control life affect your relationships with other people?

_____

_____

_____

7) What do you think it means to give God control?

_____

_____

_____

You trust that God has your best interest at heart and that He is ultimately in control anyway. You realize that no matter how hard you try you can never truly be in control of anything other than your own thoughts, feelings, and actions. You recognize that you cannot be perfect, and life is not perfect. Believe that when you release your burdens to God He is taking care of them and give Him control of each situation instead of trying to control it yourself.

Remember you are not going to be a puppet when you give God control!

JOURNAL

JOURNAL Week Four Day Six

_____
_____
_____
_____
_____
_____
_____
_____
_____
_____
_____
_____
_____
_____
_____
_____
_____
_____
_____
_____
_____
_____
_____
_____
_____
_____
_____
_____
_____
_____
_____
_____
_____
_____
_____

TRUST AND CONTROL

TRUST AND CONTROL

TIME FOR ACTION
Week Four Day Seven

☐ I commit to recognize God as my perfect Heavenly Father who will never let me down or abandon me

☐ I commit to learning to trust God and allowing people to earn my trust

☐ I commit to breaking down the walls that alienate me and to build healthy boundaries

☐ I commit to accept the help my Heavenly Father offers me even if it's through other people

☐ I commit to stop trying to be in control of everything and to give God control

On the next page, write about how this chapter has impacted you. Are you able to let God take the position of Father in your life? If not, what is keeping you from allowing that to happen?

TRUST AND CONTROL

JOURNAL

_____

_____

_____

_____

_____

_____

_____

_____

_____

_____

_____

_____

_____

_____

_____

_____

_____

_____

_____

_____

_____

_____

_____

_____

_____

_____

_____

_____

_____

_____

_____

_____

_____

TRUST AND CONTROL

CHAPTER FIVE

TO DO

Week Five:

Day One
- ☐ Read the Intro
- ☐ Do the Study Questions
- ☐ Journal

Day Two
- ☐ Read, Healing from Guilt and Shame
- ☐ Do the Study Questions
- ☐ Journal

Day Three
- ☐ Read, Bind up the Lies of the Enemy
- ☐ Do the Study Questions
- ☐ Journal

Day Four
- ☐ Read, Break Free from Bondages
- ☐ Do the Study Questions
- ☐ Journal

Day Five
- ☐ Journal

Day Six
- ☐ Journal

Day Seven
- ☐ Time for Action
- ☐ Journal

Chapter 5
FINDING FREEDOM
Week Five Day One

Guilt and shame had become such an integral part of my life that I could not separate who I was from how I felt about myself. I could not look people in the eyes without feeling as though they could see deep inside, at all the horrible details of my past. People say that the eyes are the windows to the soul and I imagined that everyone could see past my crumbling facade and into the dark, sad person that I really was inside. At the same time, however, I felt like nobody really knew me because I was hiding so much of who I was as a result of guilt and shame.

Part of the healing process required that I discover who I truly was, apart from what had happened to me in the past. Although over 20 years had gone by since being raped and abused, it still affected me like it was yesterday and it had a negative impact on my self image. I had to realize that the events of my past do not define who I am, and I alone, have the power to choose how they affect my life. I needed to learn to silence the thoughts of guilt and shame that went on inside my head over and over.

"You were sexually abused!" SHAME!
"You did not protect yourself!" GUILT!
"You were raped!" SHAME!
"You did not remain pure for your husband!" GUILT!

I could go on and on about the things that reverberated inside my head. The lies that I had believed about myself not only empowered guilt and shame but also allowed them to control how I felt, until one evening when my husband and I were in the middle of a disagreement. The heat of the argument spurred my husband to reference some of my past decisions, things that I had serious shame about. I ran outside and locked myself in the car, crying hysterically. It was at that moment that I realized how crippled I had become by these self-destructive thoughts, and so I cried out to God and begged him to take away the guilt and shame. I just could not deal with it anymore; I needed deep healing. In that painful, yet intimate time with God, I found release from both guilt and shame. In that time alone with my Father in Heaven, I was vulnerable, I was honest, and I was desperately humble. I revealed my heart to Him and my need for His help. This was not something I could do alone, I needed Him and only Him to remove my guilt and shame, and I made the decision, that instant, to release it to Him.

STUDY

1) What is causing your guilt and shame?

_____

_____

_____

2) How has guilt and shame affected your life?

_____

_____

the inability to accept forgiveness, difficulty drawing close to people, afraid people can see right through you

3) How does it affect your self image?

_____

_____

_____

you have negative self talk, you despise yourself, you lack confidence

4) How does guilt and shame limit your ability to draw close to people and develop healthy relationships?

_____

_____

_____

JOURNAL

HEALING FROM GUILT AND SHAME
Week Five Day Two

What is your internal voice telling you? Are you struggling with guilt and shame? Don't get me wrong, I'm not saying that there isn't a time and a place for guilt and shame. Obviously, they can make us aware of things that we should not have done, and hopefully prompt us to repent of wrong choices. However, God does not want us to be enslaved by guilt and shame, nor does He want us to be alienated by these feelings. He came to set us free from guilt and shame through the cleansing power of His blood and the forgiveness that comes with it. God wants to use us to do His will, but we cannot do that if we are struggling to find freedom for ourselves and are unable to be set free from the shackles of guilt and shame.

You've heard the phrase, "the blind leading the blind," the meaning becomes very clear when you think of it in this context. If you are unable to accept the freedom of the forgiveness offered to you through the blood sacrifice of Christ Jesus, and you are a slave to guilt and shame, how can you share the gospel with someone else who needs it and help them find freedom from guilt and shame? It is the blind leading the blind, isn't it?

When a mother tries to get her child to try a new food, the first thing she does is show the child that she has tasted it and how good she thinks it is. I don't think she would have much luck if she said to her child, "I don't like broccoli, but here, you should eat it because I'm sure you will like it and it is so good for you." She would not be very convincing in that situation. She needs to lead by example. She needs to experience and enjoy the flavor of broccoli before she can ever expect her child to give even a moment of thought to trying it. The child, after seeing that the mother has enjoyed it, will then be more receptive to the possibility that broccoli would be something good to eat.

It is the same way with ministering to a hurting individual, they are not going to believe that they can be released from guilt and shame, and find healing, if you are still held captive by it.

Your healing is going to be a great testimony to the people around you, and that thought should motivate you to work hard at releasing guilt and shame. It is a choice only you can make, accept that you are forgiven and allow the knowledge of forgiveness to release you from the shackles of guilt and shame once and for all.

STUDY

1) How can you remove guilt and shame from your life?

make the "choice" to release your guilt and shame to God, accept the forgiveness offered, ask God to help you break free from guilt and shame, recognize that some things were out of your control and you should not be ashamed of them

2) Who has the power to choose the effect the past has on your life and who you are?

only you have the power to choose the effect the past has on your life, your past does not define you

FINDING FREEDOM

3) Have you been able to fully accept God's forgiveness?

_____

4) How does it make you feel to know that the forgiveness God offers you also covers the things that cause you guilt and shame?

_____
_____
_____

5) Have you asked God to release you from guilt and shame and have you made the choice to release them?

_____

6) What obstacles are keeping you from finding freedom from guilt and shame?

_____
_____
_____
_____
_____

JOURNAL

BIND UP THE LIES OF THE ENEMY
Week Five Day Three

The lies of the enemy can be very convincing and seem to be intensely powerful. Nevertheless, we have to give him the power to deceive us; he does not have that power innately.

In order to deceive, all the devil has to do is entice a person to listen to his lies and then convince them that his lies are reality. Once he has that power over a person he can tell them anything he desires and they will believe it.

The reality is we are each given the truth through the word of God. Anything that we hear or perceive that goes against what the word of God states is, in fact, a deceptive lie of the enemy.

One thing you will need to learn is that the internal voice you hear speaking deceptive, destructive words about you is not of God. These thoughts and words can be lies that you perpetuate from childhood memories or feelings of incompetency. You may be hearing lies such as; "you are not good enough," "nobody loves you," "you're ugly," "you are not needed or wanted," "you can't accomplish anything," "nobody would care if you were gone," or "you can't do anything right," none of these thoughts are truthful or Godly.

The deceiver, Satan, will also try to convince you to take on guilt and shame again, so be aware of the thought patterns that have gone along with those feelings so that you won't be ensnared by them again.

The fact is, these thought patterns are traps set for you by the deceiver himself. He only needs to put the thought in your mind through either circumstances or events, and then continually remind you of these feelings until you believe them to be truth. Once you have bought into the lie, he doesn't have to do much of anything more because you will begin to say these things to yourself. His job is done; the destruction becomes your own doing.

In reality, all that we have to do to defeat his plan is believe the words that God speaks about us. "For though we live in the world, we do not wage war as the world does. The weapons we fight with are not the weapons of the world. On the contrary, they have divine power to demolish strongholds. We demolish arguments and every pretension that sets itself up against the knowledge of God, and we take captive every thought to make it obedient to Christ" (2 Cor. 10:3-5).

In order to take captive every thought, I would suggest that you write down the typical phrases that you hear, and then contrast them with a piece of scripture that states the biblical truth. Keep this paper with you so that whenever you start to hear these deceptive phrases, you will have the weapon to combat those words on hand and ready to use. At first, it will not be easy to bring those scripture verses to mind, but after some time, you will have them memorized and you won't necessarily need the paper any more. Those positive thoughts from the bible will take precedence over the negative thoughts and truth will prevail. Remember to take every thought captive!

STUDY

---

1) List some of the negative phrases you hear in your thoughts.

_____

_____

_____

_____

_____

_____

_____

_____

2) Do you remember the first time you heard these things? Where did those thoughts come from?

_____

_____

_____

_____

3) Who says these things to you now?

_____

4) Are the things you hear about yourself truthful or are they lies?

_____

5) How can you take captive every thought?

_____

contrast the negative lies of the enemy with the positive words of scripture, believe the truth rather than the lie

Make a list of scriptures that contrast the lies you have believed about yourself. Ask your mentor for help if you need it.

_____

_____

_____

_____

_____

JOURNAL

_____

_____

_____

_____

_____

_____

_____

_____

_____

_____

_____

_____

_____

_____

_____

_____

_____

_____

_____

_____

_____

_____

_____

_____

_____

_____

_____

_____

_____

_____

_____

_____

_____

_____

_____

BREAK FREE FROM BONDAGES
Week Five Day Four

Once you stop believing the lies of the enemy, you can be empowered to break free from the bondages that have controlled your life. I touched on this subject earlier in this book, but I feel it is important to go over this topic again at this time. The reason for revisiting this is because I noticed a pattern as I worked with the girls in my youth group. It seems as though in the beginning of the healing process, the motivation to find healing allows a person to break free from the habits that they use to cover up their pain, by the methods mentioned earlier in this book. However, as things get deeper into the healing process, the tendency is to revert back to the "comfortable" coping mechanisms. It is a painful revelation to the individual who had thought they had gained victory over this bondage and also to the person who is acting as spiritual mentor. It can feel like a failure, but it isn't.

If this happens to you and you revert back to past behaviors, feelings, or thought processes (including unforgiveness), look at it as an opportunity to really prove to yourself that you can gain final victory over this bondage. You are a stronger person! You are an individual who knows their true potential! You know that God loves you and has better plans for your life! This is your moment to shine and to make the informed decision to stop, once and for all, the destructive actions that have controlled your life for so long. This is your choice and no one else's.

I remember when one of the girls in my small group called me and began to tell me about how she was slipping back into past destructive behaviors. I explained to her that I had done all that I could do, I taught her what her tools were, showed her the truth in God's Word, and that it was now up to her to make the decision to break free once and for all. She needed to make the decision for herself, not for me or anyone else. I expressed to her how concerned I was for her and how I wanted her to gain final victory.

I used the following analogy, "It is like I taught you everything you need to know in order to drive safely, by keeping both of your hands on the wheel and your eyes on the road, always being aware of your surroundings and what is going on around you.

"Then one day, you call me while you are driving and you say, 'Guess what! I'm driving blindfolded and I don't have my hands on the steering wheel!'"

I explained, "I am helpless, there is nothing I can do to help you, I am not even in the car with you. You know what you need to do; you have all the knowledge that can keep you safe, it is up to you to 'choose' to make the right decisions. I cannot make you take the blindfold off, and I cannot make you take hold of the steering wheel, only you can make that choice."

As you can probably understand, I felt very helpless as her mentor. However, I knew that I had equipped her with the tools that she can use for the rest of her life, and I needed to allow her the chance to make the right choice for herself. She is an adult now and I am very proud of the changes that she has made so far. I know that there is still a lot of healing that needs to take place in her life, but I am also aware that healing is a lifelong process.

Just like the girl in the story, the choice is now yours. You have the tools to break free from bondages! Make the choice to do what is right and be who you deserve to be; who God wants you to be.

We all have to make a daily choice to live free from the guilt, shame, lies, and bondages that have kept us trapped. Make the choice now, to live victoriously!

STUDY

Before answering these questions, take a moment to review all of the past lessons in this book and consider all that you've learned so far.

1) What behaviors, feelings, or thought processes have you reverted back to that you need to break free from once and for all?

2) What have you learned about yourself while going through this book?

3) Are you a stronger person and do you realize that you have the power to make the right choices? Why or Why not?

4) What is still keeping you from breaking free?

5) How can you stop falling back into those destructive coping mechanisms?

_____

_____

_____

_____

make the choice to do something different, use what you have learned, use a new healthy coping mechanism

6) What are some of the new healthy coping mechanisms you have discovered since doing this study?

_____

_____

_____

_____

_____

take a walk, have a quiet time with God, journal, talk to your safe person, read your bible, pray, spend time in praise and worship

JOURNAL

JOURNAL Week Five Day Five

JOURNAL Week Five Day Six

_____

_____
_____
_____
_____
_____
_____
_____
_____
_____
_____
_____
_____
_____
_____
_____
_____
_____
_____
_____
_____
_____
_____
_____
_____
_____
_____
_____
_____
_____
_____
_____

_____
_____
_____
_____
_____
_____
_____
_____
_____
_____
_____
_____
_____
_____
_____
_____
_____
_____
_____
_____
_____
_____
_____
_____
_____
_____
_____
_____
_____
_____
_____
_____
_____
_____

TIME FOR ACTION
Week Five Day Seven

- ☐ I commit to break free from guilt and shame
- ☐ I commit to replace the negative lies of the enemy with the truth of God's Word
- ☐ I commit to stop perpetuating the negative thoughts about myself
- ☐ I commit to make the choice to be completely victorious over the bondages of the past

On the next page, write down any thoughts that you want to share, lessons that you have learned, or revelations of truth you've had about yourself.

JOURNAL

_____

_____
_____
_____
_____
_____
_____
_____
_____
_____
_____
_____
_____
_____
_____
_____
_____
_____
_____
_____
_____
_____
_____
_____
_____
_____
_____
_____
_____
_____
_____
_____
_____
_____
_____

CHAPTER SIX

TO DO

Week Six:

Day One
- ☐ Read the Intro
- ☐ Do the Study Questions
- ☐ Journal

Day Two
- ☐ Read, Be Victorious
- ☐ Do the Study Questions
- ☐ Journal

Day Three
- ☐ Read, Finding Purpose for Your Pain
- ☐ Do the Study Questions
- ☐ Journal

Day Four
- ☐ Read, Healing is a Lifelong Process
- ☐ Do the Study Questions
- ☐ Journal

Day Five
- ☐ Read, Don't Let the Busyness of Life Distract You
- ☐ Do the Study Questions
- ☐ Journal

Day Six
- ☐ Journal

Day Seven
- ☐ Time for Action
- ☐ Journal

Chapter 6
SMALL VICTORIES, HOW TO KEEP THEM
Week Six Day One

Several years ago, I began to journal during my prayer time. I use my journal as a way to put my thoughts down on paper and to help me communicate with God my struggles, feelings, and weaknesses. It helps me stay focused and feel like I have really given these things up to God. It's my way of giving God control over my circumstances, and it helps me keep track of my prayer requests.

The interesting thing about journaling is that you can look back over time and be reminded of how far you have come in your healing process and at the same time recognize the answer to previous prayers once they come to pass, (Sometimes, we make the request but forget to give God the glory when He answers). I love seeing His purposes unfold in my journal, as I begin to see a map, so to speak, come to life.

The following is one of my own (unedited) journal entries

from Feb. 20, 2005...

"'Threshold of Change,' that was the word that I received today. I have been struggling today with memories of the past. Memories of what I could've done or should've done. For the past 20 years I have had to deal with the guilt, shame, and memories of the things in my past. Today I asked Bob to pray for me, I told him last week about most of the details and asked him to forgive me. I wish that I could have talked about this a lot sooner than this. It feels so good to be free from this secret. I just wish that I could be freed from the memories of it. It seems Satan uses it to remind me of my imperfections and loves to take me back to the past. I still feel that same insecurity and naivety that I felt then. Every time I think of the rape, (that word is so hard to write), I return to that place again. Sixteen/ Seventeen, lonely, abandoned, unloved, insecure, stupid, vulnerable, helpless, hopeless, suicidal, desiring to be loved, feeling like nothing, empty, hurting, wanting to love but hating the world, and always trying to fill the void place.

"I shared with Bob that the word I got today spoke of two things to me. The first is where I was the day that I committed my life to Christ. I was at a place in my life that if change didn't occur, I had nothing to live for. The second being where I am right now. God has brought me to this place, the 'threshold of change.' I know that through all this 'cleansing' that has taken place over this last year, God is going to carry me across the threshold like a groom does his bride. I am so eager for what He has in store for me.

"Dear God,
I pray that you would help me to forgive myself for the sins of my past, for not guarding this temple of yours, for not protecting my purity. God, I break all the soul ties that have been formed. I bind my marriage and claim it as pure and claim a holy soul tie between Bob and I, a soul tie that you, God alone have created. I bind up the lies of the enemy and claim that I am victorious over the past, that I am a changed, reborn child of God, and that the sins of my past are washed away by the blood of the Lamb, the perfect sacrifice. I am no longer in debt because my debts have been paid. I praise you Lord Jesus, that I am new! I am pure in your sight!

"Thank you for loving me into a new place, that you have changed me ever so gently. Thank you for being patient and never forsaking me.

"In Jesus name, Amen."

One and a half years after this journal entry was written, work on this book began. Although I did not understand the full implications of that statement, the "threshold of change" came to represent the healing that had been taking place which would finally allow me to share my story. As I go back in my journal and read what I've written over the years, I gain a whole new perspective on my past and I appreciate all the more, God's hand in my healing.

STUDY

1) How has journaling helped you during this study?

_____

_____

_____

2) In what ways do you see journaling becoming a part of your daily life?

_____

_____

_____

3) What obstacles will keep you from continuing to journal, or what obstacles have kept you from journaling during this study?

_____

_____

_____

4) In what ways could your journaling help other people?

_____

_____

_____

learning to clearly communicate your testimony, revealing how God has worked through your circumstances, maybe using your journal to write a book someday

JOURNAL

BE VICTORIOUS
Week Six Day Two

God is capable of seeing the past, present, and future of our life map. We tend to only see the present and the present can sometimes be infiltrated by the past. Our limited visibility can make us feel like we have lost our victory especially when the past begins to creep back into the present through thoughts, emotions, and behaviors. As the old saying goes, two steps forward and one step back. The healing process can feel that way at times. The thing to remember is that it is still forward progress even though it may not always feel like it.

One of the students in my youth group always struggled with keeping her victories, as I called them, things that she had gained understanding from or had learned to overcome. She kept anticipating one big event where she would miraculously find complete healing. Instead she kept having smaller revelations of truth. Those revelations were still victories but they just never seemed to be enough for her, so instead of being thankful for the small victories, she tended to throw them back and revert to previous thought processes. She really struggled with whether or not she would ever find healing.

To help this student understand what she was doing, I shared this analogy with her. I said, "Two men are rowing out to sea, they both leave at the same time of day, they both have the same boat and equipment, with equal opportunity to catch fish. The first man catches a fish and thinks to himself, 'this one is too small.' So he throws the fish back in the water and he continues to do so, fish after fish, with the intention of catching 'the big one.' The second man has about the same luck as he is catching the same sized fish; however, he decides to keep them. At the end of the day, the two men return to shore. The first man has caught several hundreds of fish but returns with an empty boat because, in his opinion, the fish just weren't big enough, and he wanted to catch 'the big one.' The second man could hardly keep his boat afloat because his boat was full to overflowing with fish. The second man recognized that each fish had value, no matter the size, and he knew that several small fish were more valuable than one big fish."

This is what healing is like; you may not have instant healing. Healing is something that takes time and comes in layers and steps. You may find victory over one thing and then go several months before finding victory over another. Look at those times in-between as an opportunity for you to rest, recover, and prepare for the next step. You also need to truly learn to live with the newly gained victory. If the healing process goes too fast you may forget what you have learned. Take the time to really apply the things you learn to your life. Then, when you are ready, you can move on to the next step in the journey.

Journaling will help you see how far you have come and also help to motivate you and keep you on track. Use your journal to write down the things you have learned and the victories you have gained. Also, journal the areas that you know you need to work on and ask God to help you work on those things when the time is right.

Remember, the small victories are worth keeping and you can be victorious!

SMALL VICTORIES, HOW TO KEEP THEM

STUDY

---

1) How do you think God's ability to see the entirety of your life affects His decision to allow certain events to happen?

_____

_____

He works all things out for the good of those who love Him. He is able to see how things will affect all people. He may allow something to happen to you because He knows you will learn something from it and in turn help someone else.

When the Bible says that He works things out for the good of those who love Him (Rom. 8:28), it is not just referring to you; it is talking about all those who love Him. For that very reason, some things may not seem to be for your good; it may be that it is for the good of others. Keeping that in mind, begin to look at every situation as a learning opportunity. In that way, you can turn the bad things in your life into a positive learning experience which, in turn, will allow you to help others going through a similar situation ultimately giving your pain a purpose.

2) Do you still feel like the past is keeping you from gaining victory? If so, in what ways?

_____

_____

3) Share ways that your past continues to creep into the present.

_____

fear, lack of trust, insecurities, bad memories, flash backs

SMALL VICTORIES, HOW TO KEEP THEM

4) In the story of the two fishermen, which man are you? The man who keeps all the fish, or the one who throws them all back?

_____

5) What victories are you keeping?

_____

_____

(you may have stopped repeating negative thoughts to yourself, stopped self-destructive behavior, or forgiven yourself)

6) What victories are you rejecting and in what ways are you throwing those victories back?

_____

_____

(reverting to old habits or thought patterns)

7) Why do you reject the small victories?

_____

they may seem unimportant, too insignificant to matter in the big picture of the healing journey

8) How will journaling help you keep the small victories?

_____

as you learn a new lesson write it down, read over past entries to remind yourself of these lessons

SMALL VICTORIES, HOW TO KEEP THEM

JOURNAL

SMALL VICTORIES, HOW TO KEEP THEM

FINDING PURPOSE FOR YOUR PAIN
Week Six Day Three

Part of the healing process is discovering a purpose for your suffering. No one wants to feel that they have suffered in vain. What good would that do? As I shared in an earlier chapter, something I tend to do when I am going through a tough time is ask God, "What do you want me to learn from this?" You can do the same thing with experiences from your past; you can still seek to learn from them. I would say that learning from your circumstances is the most important key to accomplishing the task of finding a purpose for the situations you have found yourself in.

One of the advantages of learning to talk about your pain, finding forgiveness, and achieving freedom from guilt and shame, is that you gain the ability to talk openly to more people about your testimony. Your testimony in itself, can impact and change lives. By revealing God's truth and what you have been able to learn from your experiences, and through sharing your own story of healing, God can reveal Himself and His desire to heal the person hearing it. Again, it is like the child trying broccoli, "if it is good for you mom, then I guess it would be good for me." Your testimony can help another individual realize that it is ok to ask for help, it is ok to reveal weaknesses; it is ok to talk about it.

Hearing your story can be the first step to healing for someone else. Sometimes it can be a matter of simple validation. A hurting person desires to know that he or she is not alone in their suffering, and that there is hope. They may not be able to see hope on their own. Your testimony can demonstrate hope in a real, tangible way. This is one way to give your pain purpose. What an incredible way to become victorious over the plans of the enemy. This again, is where journaling can come in handy. If you can journal your feelings then it will help you to express them to others with more ease. Don't be ashamed, be victorious! Share your testimony, it is unique, no one else has a story like yours and who better to tell it than you.

STUDY

1) In what ways are you able to give your pain purpose?

_____

_____

helping others in similar situations, sharing your testimony of healing

2) On a separate piece of paper, write out your testimony, include lessons you have learned, and victories gained. **Leaders: you may want to ask a few small group members to share their testimony.**

3) How has God facilitated healing in your life?

_____

_____

_____

_____

_____

JOURNAL

HEALING IS A LIFELONG PROCESS
Week Six Day Four

By now you are hopefully noticing a change in your life and seeing some positive results from doing this study. You have probably found some healing already and you may feel pretty good about that. However, life does not stand still once you find healing, in other words you will still have things happen to you in life that will require you to revisit the steps you've learned during this study. And don't forget that we're all in a process of healing, and each of us are at a different stage of healing, even if it is denial. Recognizing this will help you show grace to people who do hurtful things to you. Think of life as a constant healing opportunity, not just for you but also for those around you. Look at it this way; every day, for the rest of your life, you will have to use the lessons taught in these chapters, those learned in counseling, and the truth learned from the Bible, in order to cope with the day to day challenges that will be presented to you.

Healing is a daily choice. Every day you will have to "choose" to be victorious, "choose" to forgive, "choose" to give God control, and "choose" to break free from the lies and bondages of the past. You ARE equipped and capable of making the decision to drive without a blindfold and with both hands on the wheel!

While healing truly is a choice, maintaining hope and motivation can sometimes be a challenge and you will need some ways to keep on "growing in the right direction." The following are some tools that you have at your disposal that will help you continue to defeat the enemy, continue to draw near to God, and continue to learn, grow, and heal. In that way it will also help you stay motivated and hopeful.

Here are your basic tools...

The Word of God, The Bible: Use this to replace lies with truth, to learn more about God and how much He loves you. You will learn to know Him as your Heavenly Father, and to attain revelation to break free from the sins that hold you captive. You should read as often as you possibly can. Don't forget to write down on a piece of paper the lies that you tend to hear contrasted with the truth found in God's word, and keep it with you.

Worship and Praise: Find some worship music and use this to sing praises to God showing Him how grateful you are for the healing that He has given you and for the continued healing that is still to come. Show Him how humbled you are that He loves you enough to have sent His Son to die on the cross for you personally. Tell Him how much you love Him in return. I also like to sleep with worship music because it helps me to stay focused on God even when I am dreaming. Praise Him in the good and the bad, even when you don't feel like it. Give Him the glory in all things and remember to thank Him for answered prayers.

And most importantly...

Prayer and intimacy or quiet time with God: Use quiet time to draw near to God, to speak to Him and allow Him to speak to you. Begin to journal during this time. It helps to have a place that you set aside in your home for this so that you have a normal routine. Let this time be used to give God complete control of all aspects of your life, it should be a time of intimacy and holding nothing back from Him.

SMALL VICTORIES, HOW TO KEEP THEM

Prayer is also something you should do all day long by "practicing the presence of God," in other words, remind yourself that He is always with you so you can talk to Him any time you think about it. Prayer doesn't have to mean bowing your head and folding your hands, it could mean just talking to him like you talk to the people around you or on the phone, of course you may want to pray silently otherwise people may think you are talking to yourself! Get the idea of typical prayer out of your mind and start to actually communicate with God. This will build you up and strengthen you when you are struggling during your day. Remember to totally rely on God.

STUDY

1) What are some choices you have made in order to change your present circumstances?

   change friendships, stop tempting activities, be more respectful to your people in authority, choose forgiveness, got out of an abusive situation

2) What are some things you can do to maintain motivation, hope, and continue the healing process?

   read your bible, journal, worship and praise God, have prayer and intimate times with God

3) How do you practice the presence of God? What does it mean?

   remember that God is always with you so you can talk to Him any time you want

SMALL VICTORIES, HOW TO KEEP THEM

JOURNAL

_____

_____
_____
_____
_____
_____
_____
_____
_____
_____
_____
_____
_____
_____
_____
_____
_____
_____
_____
_____
_____
_____
_____
_____
_____
_____
_____
_____
_____
_____
_____
_____
_____
_____

DON'T LET THE BUSYNESS OF LIFE DISTRACT YOU
Week Six Day Five

As you finish this book and continue on your path toward healing, you may find yourself getting distracted with the busyness of life. I've seen it happen many times before. Every day life takes precedence over healing sometimes and that's ok, just be ready to start the process again when things slow down for you.

One of my students began to feel really good about life after she found some healing. Honestly, it had been a very long time since she had felt that good. As a result, she became very passionate about ministry and started serving in many different areas. In the process, she lost focus of her own healing as she filled her life with several time consumers and became distracted by all her commitments. Her healing was put on the back burner at that point.

God gave me a word of encouragement that I shared with her. The word was, "As things begin to slow down for you, more stuff will start coming to the surface and you need to be prepared to work through them. Don't get bombarded by it, just see the downtime as an opportunity to continue the healing process."

She did, in fact, have a time where things slowed down for her and she had to work through some more healing during that time period.

I have also experienced this same scenario in my own healing process. A recent move took me out of ministry for a short period of time and I found it was God's intention that more healing was to happen for me during that time. This type of healing was not able to happen when I was busy being focused on ministry. I needed to be able to focus my attention on just myself and not students or prayer ministry. During this time, I learned more about myself and afterward I was more energized to do what God wanted me to do.

When life gets busy for you, remember that there is still healing that has to happen for you, and when time allows for it let the healing continue. You will always be learning, growing, and healing. Don't be afraid of it and don't let it discourage you. Remember, healing is a lifelong process and it comes in layers, steps, and times of rest and release. Be ready for all that God has in store for you and remember that God has better plans for you!

STUDY

1) What activities cause you to get so busy that you stop working on healing or drawing close to God?

_____

_____

_____

2) What should you do during those busy times?

_____

_____

Always remember, there will be more time to heal when life slows down for you. Don't get discouraged when things start to surface in those quiet moments.

SMALL VICTORIES, HOW TO KEEP THEM

JOURNAL

_____

_____
_____
_____
_____
_____
_____
_____
_____
_____
_____
_____
_____
_____
_____
_____
_____
_____
_____
_____
_____
_____
_____
_____
_____
_____
_____
_____
_____
_____
_____
_____

SMALL VICTORIES, HOW TO KEEP THEM

JOURNAL Week Six Day Six

_____

_____

_____

_____

_____

_____

_____

_____

_____

_____

_____

_____

_____

_____

_____

_____

_____

_____

_____

_____

_____

_____

_____

_____

_____

_____

_____

_____

_____

_____

_____

_____

_____

_____

TIME FOR ACTION
Week Six Day Seven

☐ I commit to keep the small victories

☐ I commit to continue to journal

☐ I commit to share my testimony so that others may be blessed

☐ I commit to recognize that there is a purpose for my pain

☐ I commit to understanding that healing is a life long process

☐ I commit to use my basic tools, the bible, praise and worship, and prayer to learn, grow, and heal

☐ I commit to believing that God has better plans for me!

On the next page, answer the questions, What have I learned about myself during the course of this book? How can I learn to share my testimony?

JOURNAL

<u>Final Thoughts</u>

As a final thought, I wanted to share with you more details about the woman in chapter one. I kept her nameless in the beginning because it really would not have added any significance to the text at that moment. However, out of respect for her and because I want to dedicate this book to her, I would like to share a bit about who that woman was.

She was my mother, and she was the woman who attempted suicide. My mother was a woman of strength, compassion, and love. She was stern, determined, and a strict disciplinarian. She endured much of the same abuse that I went through as a child. Her story and mine were similar in many ways. She had a stepfather who was sexually abusive. She had a mother who didn't know how to deal with it and so my mother also ended up on her own at 16. She felt abandoned and unloved. Her mother also stayed with her stepfather even though the stepfather had committed such crimes against my mother and her siblings.

Here is where our stories differ. My mother got pregnant at 16 and married an abusive husband, my biological father. Through his hands she also endured much. She told stories of how she was raped, abused, and ridiculed by him. She had three children by my father, divorced him and married two other times.

Her final husband, my stepfather, sexually abused each of us girls. Throughout their marriage my stepfather was unfaithful to my mother with many women but she continued to remain with him because she saw so much good in him. It was during one of these affairs that my mother decided to take her own life.

My mother had spent the majority of her life being angry at God and blaming Him for all the bad things that she had went through. The miracle of her liver being healed and her life restored is what allowed her to finally forgive God and to find hope. The reality was that God used this pain to bring her to a place of forgiveness and reconciliation to Him.

My mother ended up living to love God for the remaining two years of her life. She was baptized in October of 2008 and she passed away on May 31st, 2009, from emphysema. I still miss her terribly, but I know that I will get to see her again someday and will spend eternity with her in heaven. I attribute a lot of who I am to who she was and the strength that she showed me during her lifetime. She was not perfect, but she was my mother, and I love her.

Pictured above: The Author, Crystal Deeds
and her Mother, Carol Smith in 2005.

This book is dedicated to you Mom!

References

Chapter 1
[1]Taken from The Problem of Pain by C.S. Lewis
ISBN 978-0-06-194764-3 Copyright © 1940 by C.S. Lewis Pte.
Ltd. Copyright restored © 1996 by C.S. Lewis Pte. Ltd. Used by
permission of HarperCollins Publishers. www.harpercollins.com
pg. 66

[2]Taken from Safe People by Dr. Henry Cloud and Dr. John
Townsend ISBN-10: 0-310-21084-4 Copyright © 1995 by Henry
Cloud and John Townsend. Used by permission of Zondervan.
www.zondervan.com pg. 143

Chapter 2
[1]Please note that the method of evangelism used here is based on
"The Way of the Master" ISBN-978-0-88270-220-9 Copyright ©
2006 by Ray Comfort, which is an excellent resource for anyone
who has a desire to help save the lost.

[2]Taken from God's Remedy for Rejection by Derek Prince
ISBN-13: 978-0-88368-864-9 Copyright © 1993 by Derek Prince
Ministries, International. Used by permission of Whitaker
House. www.whitakerhouse.com pg.38

Chapter 3
[1]"I'm Still Learning to Forgive" by Corrie Ten Boom is
reproduced with permission from *Guideposts* magazine,
Guideposts.org. Copyright © by Guideposts. All rights reserved.

[2]Quote from C.S. Lewis source unknown

Acknowledgements

I would like to express my unending gratitude to God, my Heavenly Father, for saving me and giving me the hope necessary to live my life in pursuit of the healing only He could provide, and for helping me to discover the plans He has for my life.

God, I will always love you and I will serve you with all of my heart and soul until the day I breathe my last!

I would like to give credit to Pastor Keith Boyer, Former Lead Pastor of Crossroads Community Church and Jon Eastlick, Outreach Pastor of Crossroads Community Church. Many lessons were learned through their teaching and I have shared some of those lessons throughout this book.

I would also like to thank the many people who helped me with this project. I especially want to thank my husband Bob who stood by me throughout the healing process, my daughter Hannah who has always been such an amazing young lady, and my son, Steven for his talent in helping with all of the graphic design projects, not to mention the endless hours of planning, design and marketing advice! Thank you to Aubrey Harper, for designing the cover layout, and Missy Culpepper for her editing advice. To the girls who allowed me to photograph them for the cover, I love how perfectly it turned out! Finally, I give many thanks to those who helped with financing, and those who simply prayed and offered me their support. I could not have accomplished this task without each and every one of you!

Recommended Resources

RAINN: Rape, Abuse, and Incest National Network
    http://www.rainn.org/
    1-800-656-HOPE
National Suicide Prevention Lifeline
    http://www.suicidepreventionlifeline.org/
    Need help? In the U.S., call 1-800-273-8255
Al-Anon/Alateen Hotline
    Hope & Help for young people who are the relatives &
    friends of a problem drinker. http://www.al-
    anon.alateen.org/
    1-800-344-2666
Alcohol/Drug Abuse Hotline
    1-800-662-HELP
Child Abuse Hotline
    1-800-4-A-CHILD (1-800-422-4453)
Domestic Violence Hotline
    1-800-799-SAFE (1-800-799-7233)
Eating Disorders Awareness and Prevention
    1-800-931-2237 (Hours: 8am-noon daily, PT)
Eating Disorders Center
    1-888-236-1188
Homeless/Runaway National Runaway Hotline
    800-231-6946
Incest Awareness Foundation
    1-888-547-3222
AACC: American Association of Christian Counselors
    http://www.aacc.net/resources/find-a-counselor/
H.O.P.E. Ministries
www.betterplansfor.me

APPENDIX A
Confidentiality Agreement for Small Group

This book, when used in a small group setting, is an opportunity for people to share and deal with real issues that include their personal information. Therefore, confidentiality in small groups must be maintained.

I _____(participant) acknowledge that keeping confidentiality means that all group members agree not to pass on personal or private information whether it is shared before, during, or after small group meetings, without the permission of the person who shared the information. I realize that I may hear sensitive testimonies dealing with serious issues of a personal nature. I also understand this agreement is for my benefit as well so that I can feel safe enough to be authentic with those around me.

I fully recognize the only exceptions to breaking confidentiality would be if I have reason to believe that someone is in danger, or has become a danger to themselves. In such circumstances, I pledge to bring this information to my group leader and trust that they will do what they feel is best for the situation. As a participant, I understand that the group leader may make the decision to bring in outside help if they feel it is necessary to keep me safe, or to facilitate further healing and growth, this, of course, will be with my knowledge and participation if possible. I agree to do what is necessary to grow personally throughout this study, and to recognize that it is me who makes the choice to heal and as such I trust the judgment of my leader to do what is right for my personal situation.

By signing below, I agree to keep all information heard at small group, or at times in between meetings completely confidential as outlined above.

_____   _____

(Participant Signature)   (Date)

APPENDIX B

Sample Parental Agreement for Church Sponsored Youth Groups
(due to the sensitive nature of the subject matter you may find it necessary to have the parents agree to allow their child to participate)

Your child has expressed an interest in attending a small group study based on a book titled, "I Have Better Plans for You" by Crystal Deeds.

This study is intended to encourage and equip teens for dealing with hurts, habits, and hang-ups. Therefore, due to the sensitive nature of some of the information that may be shared by the group, each student is required to sign a confidentiality agreement which will be made available to you upon request. Because, of the sensitive nature of this study we are requiring participants to obtain permission from their parents before attending.

By signing below, you give your child, _____,
                                                        (child's name)
permission to attend a small group led by_____,
                                                        (Leader's name)
on the following days and times, _____.
I acknowledge that the Leader (will/will not) offer transportation to and/or from small group, and I release the above named Leader of any liability during small group or while traveling to and from the meeting location throughout the small group commitment.

_____
(parent's name printed)

_____   _____
(phone)   (cell)

_____   _____
(parent's signature)   (date)

Leader Contact Information _____

APPENDIX C

Sample Parental Agreement
(if not used in a Church Sponsored Youth Group)

Your child has expressed an interest in attending a small group study based on a book titled, "I Have Better Plans for You" by Crystal Deeds. This is a bible based study. However, it is not being sponsored by a church, nor is it being offered through your child's school. This is solely a private group offered on a volunteer basis.

This study is intended to encourage and equip teens for dealing with hurts, habits, and hang-ups. Therefore, due to the sensitive nature of some of the information that may be shared by the group, each student is required to sign a confidentiality agreement which will be made available to you upon request. Because, of the sensitive nature of this study we are requiring participants to obtain permission from their parents before attending.

By signing below, you give your child, _____,
(child's name)
permission to attend a small group led by_____,
(Leader's name)
on the following days and times, _____.
I acknowledge that the Leader (will/will not) offer transportation to and/or from small group, and I release the above named Leader of any liability during small group or while traveling to and from the meeting location throughout the small group commitment.

_____

(parent's name printed)

_____   _____

(phone)   (cell)

_____   _____

(parent's signature)   (date)

Leader's contact information_____

www.ingramcontent.com/pod-product-compliance
Lightning Source LLC
Chambersburg PA
CBHW051823090426
42736CB00011B/1616